SIMON & SCHUSTER BOOKS FOR YOUNG READERS
An imprint of Simon & Schuster Children's
Publishing Division
1230 Avenue of the Americas, New York, New York 10020

Book design by Russell Gordon
The text for this book is set in Aldine.
Printed in the United States of America
2 4 6 8 10 9 7 5 3 1

Library of Congress Cataloging-in-Publication Data
Mundis, Hester.
My chimp Friday : the Nana Banana chronicles / by Hester Mundis.
p. cm.
Summary: When an old friend of her father's drops off an unusually
intelligent chimpanzee at their apartment in the middle of the night
with strict orders to keep the chimp a secret, twelve-year-old Rachel
wants to know what the big mystery is all about.
ISBN 0-689-83837-9
[1. Chimpanzees—Fiction. 2. Animal intelligence—Fiction. 3. Family
life—New York (N.Y.)—Fiction. 4. New York (N.Y.)—Fiction.] I. Title.
PZ7.M92343 My 2002
[Fic]—dc21
2001042947

FIRST
EDITION

To Boris,
for sharing his world

Heartfelt thanks to the late Claire Smith for providing the
magic that made this book happen, to my agent,
Wendy Schmalz, for making the magic work, and to my
editor, David Gale, for being there to bring the magic to life.
Thanks, too, to my brother-in-law Randy VanWarmer
for keeping a smile on my face by doing what he does so
well—and to my husband, Ron VanWarmer, for absolutely
everything else.

CONTENTS

1.

One Dark and Noisy Night

The buzzing was really annoying, and Rachel was getting very angry. Ticked off big-time. Mickey Phelps—the unfunniest practical joker in the whole sixth grade (and possibly the history of the school)—had dropped an alarm clock in her backpack, and she couldn't turn it off. It sounded like the hand buzzer he had startled her with the week before. For some dumb reason she was his favorite target and his best friend. Sometimes she wondered about the "best friend" part. Yesterday in the lunchroom he had planted a grossly real-looking fake bug in her Jell-O. It was totally not funny.

Table-turning time had come.

She was just about to slip a gooey slice of pepperoni pizza under him as he was sitting down (childish but well-deserved revenge) when suddenly Mickey Phelps started to bark.

Bark?

Rachel's eyes snapped open.

The clock on her nightstand said 2:00 a.m., and someone was at the door.

The barking was coming from Wetspot, which was almost as weird as if it had come from Mickey Phelps. The Stelson family dog was the quietest (mostly) golden retriever in the history of golden retrievers. He hardly ever barked, except when Mrs. Carey, their housekeeper, turned on the vacuum cleaner. But he had a kind of dog sense when something wasn't right. And someone at the door pressing on the buzzer in the middle of the night like the building was on fire—which maybe it was—definitely wasn't right!

Rachel jumped out of bed. She went to the window, listened, and sniffed the air. No sirens, no smoke—no fire. She breathed a sigh of relief. Mr. DeFina, her homeroom teacher at The Dahl Riverside School, would have called her quick deduction "specious." He would have called it that for two reasons. One of the two reasons was that Mr. DeFina liked to use words that he believed "enriched" his students' vocabulary, and "specious"—meaning "apparently right but not necessarily so"—was an enriching favorite of his. Rachel had won last week's spelling bee and moved into the school's semifinals by getting it right (beating Mickey, who goofed on "quibbling" by using only one "b").

The other reason was that the absence of fire trucks and smoke didn't necessarily mean there couldn't be a fire somewhere in the building, and Rachel knew it. Still, specious or not, she just didn't care to think about it at the moment.

She was too curious about who was at their door.

The buzzer sounded again, followed by another uncharacteristic throaty burst from Wetspot. It was almost as if after five years of occasional "woof-woofs" he had

Hester Mundis

decided that tonight was the night to break his canine vow of silence. But then that would be just like Wetspot.

Wetspot just wasn't like other dogs. He hated rawhide chew bones, and doggie biscuits, too. He sometimes groomed himself like a cat, using his paws to clean his face and licking off anything clinging to his fur or undercarriage. He never drank from the toilet. Ever! And he *loved* broccoli. Broccoli! (Even Rachel's friend Brianne, who was trying to be a vegetarian, didn't *love* broccoli.) If his favorite pastimes weren't chasing tennis balls and Frisbees, you'd hardly think he had any dog in him at all.

In fact, Wetspot wasn't even his real name.

His real name, or at least the name he'd had at the animal shelter, was Prince. But when they'd brought him home, he wouldn't even look up when they called, "Prince!" Rachel had tried, "King," but the royal promotion didn't get his attention, either. As it turned out, he picked his own name.

It happened by accident. Well, "accidents." Whenever Rachel's younger brother, Jared, discovered that their new puppy had tinkled on the floor, he would point and announce loudly, "Wet spot!" And sure enough, the pup would come running, tail wagging. After three weeks, the wet spots no longer appeared—but the name stuck.

The buzzer sounded again, eliciting another series of barks.

"Coming, coming," Rachel's father called.

"Daddy, who's there?" Rachel asked in a loud whisper.

"Your guess is as good as mine," he whispered back as he hurried toward the apartment door, though obviously not fast enough for whoever was on the other side. There was another buzz and louder barking.

Jared came into Rachel's room. "What's going on?" he whispered.

"I don't know," she whispered, though why they were all whispering at this point was almost as much a mystery as who was at the door.

"Now, Wetspot, shhhh," her father said, "that's enough. You'll wake the whole building"—which seemed at this point to be what Wetspot had in mind.

Jared covered his ears. He had on Darth Vader pajamas, but with his thick, curly hair sticking out in different directions, he looked more like a Wookie than a Jedi warrior. "What's with Wetspot? I've never heard him like that. He sounds like Attila."

Attila was the building superintendent's dog and the most feared animal on the block—quite possibly on the whole Upper West Side. An enormous rottweiler, he had teeth that looked like a bear trap and a growl that sounded like a trapped bear. When he passed a fire hydrant he didn't lift his leg—he karate-kicked it. Mr. Aplox kept Attila on a very tight leash on walks and chained him to a post near the storage bays when he was doing work in the basement. He constantly tried to convince people—and their terrified pets—that his dog's bark was really much worse than his bite, but no one believed him.

No one, that is, except Wetspot. He and Attila were best friends.

"I think," Rachel said, "that Wetspot has just realized he's a dog. Come on!" As they went into the hall she flattened her younger brother's hair with her palm the way she remembered her mother doing.

"I'm coming, I'm coming." Ben Stelson's voice was remarkably calm considering the repeated buzzes that cut through the quiet apartment like a dentist's drill. Rachel's father was a very patient man. Her aunt Lisa swore that he had "the patience of a saint" whenever she came to stay with Rachel and Jared, and she'd stayed with them a lot in the three years since their mother had died.

Aunt Lisa was Rachel's mother's sister. She looked a little like Rachel's mother—they had the same cinnamon-colored hair and dimpled smile—which comforted Rachel. But that's where the resemblance and the comfort ended. Aunt Lisa was a royal pain in the butt.

When Aunt Lisa was around, Rachel couldn't eat anything she enjoyed without getting a totally boring lecture on how bad it was for her. Soda was "unhealthy." Fast food was "poison." And no bread in their house was ever whole-grainey enough. As far as Aunt Lisa was concerned, if you could chew it easily, it was "practically worthless," and if it tasted good, too, it was "totally worthless." She was a health nut, a neatness nut, a cleanliness nut, and totally germ-a-phobic!

The most fun Rachel had when Aunt Lisa was around was kissing Wetspot on the mouth just to see the horrified look on her aunt's face.

Oddly enough, it was not all that different from the look on the face of the man facing them when her father finally silenced the buzzing and opened their apartment door.

2.

A Mysterious Moving Bundle

Wetspot stopped barking.

Rachel and Jared stayed where they were and stared.

Standing in the doorway, tight-lipped and grimacing, was a very short, agitated man with wide, bulging eyes that gave him a permanently startled look. He wore thick, wire-rimmed glasses and had longish white hair that hung limply to the shoulders of a ridiculously large and tattered dark gray overcoat that was *sizes* too large for him; so much so that it looked to Rachel as if he had shrunk while inside it. The man's face was very pale, and he appeared to be sweating, which wasn't surprising considering the enormous coat he was wearing. What was surprising, though, was the oddly shaped blanket-wrapped bundle he was clutching.

It was moving!

Rachel inched closer.

"Why, Bucky Greene," Rachel's father stammered. "What a . . ."

Rachel hoped he wasn't going to say "pleasant surprise," although she wouldn't be surprised if he did. Her father was probably the politest man on the planet. He thanked automatic teller machines.

"What a . . . um . . . um . . ." Ben Stelson caught himself about to say what Rachel feared he was about to say and said instead, "Come in, come in. Gee, Bucky, it's been a long time. What . . . uh . . . uh . . . are you doing here . . . now? And how did you get into the building?"

Bucky Greene glanced nervously from right to left as if he were trapped in the middle of a busy intersection. "No time. No time to explain."

"Or for a visit," Rachel felt like pointing out, but didn't. She was fascinated by the bundle that now appeared to be moving across their night visitor's chest.

Jared tugged Rachel's sleeve. "What's he carrying?"

Rachel shrugged. "I haven't a clue," she whispered, "but I think we're about to find out."

"I'm sorry to get you up at this hour, Ben," Bucky apologized, "but it was the only way I could leave the lab unnoticed."

Rachel wondered how the man could go anywhere unnoticed in that ridiculously large coat.

"With the security you have over at Bio-allmeans, I'm not surprised," her father said. "But—and this may sound like a dumb question—why did you have to leave *unnoticed?*"

It didn't sound at all like a dumb question to Rachel. In fact, she edged closer to hear the answer.

"I'm afraid I can't tell you. It's"—Bucky lowered his voice—"top secret."

"TOP SECRET!"

"Not anymore," Rachel mumbled. For a biology professor who spent most of his life studying things under a microscope, her father still had a lot to learn about the Big Picture.

"Listen to me, Ben. You're a man of science as well as my friend. You're capable and you're trustworthy. And, well, quite honestly I couldn't think of anyone else to leave him with." With that, he thrust the wriggling bundle into Ben Stelson's arms.

"Him?" Rachel's father looked bewildered. "Who's *him?*"

What was him seemed a better question. Rachel leaned forward. Jared did the same.

Wetspot cocked his head.

Just then a small hand appeared from the top of the blanket and pulled it aside. There in their father's arms was a very adorable and very frightened baby chimpanzee.

"Wow! Cool!" Rachel said.

"Far out!" breathed Jared.

Wetspot made a noise that sounded as if a bark had gotten stuck in his throat.

Ben Stelson made a very similar sound. "Wait a minute, Bucky. What am I supposed to do with a—"

"Chimpanzee," said Bucky quickly. "Come on, Ben. Chimpanzees are our closest living relatives. You wouldn't turn a cousin out in the middle of the night, would you?"

He wouldn't ask that question if he knew their cousin Richard. Cousin Richard had once spent a weekend with them and crept out in the middle of the night with Rachel's dad's credit cards and the whole envelope of money she had collected for Girl Scout cookie orders. The police had come to the apartment when Richard was picked up, but her father never pressed charges. He called

Cousin Richard "the family's black sheep." Rachel called him "the family's big creep!"

"Now, Bucky, this is—"

"This is *important*," Bucky said, emphasizing the word so that there was no doubt that it was. "You *must* keep this chimp here. It'll only be for . . . oh, about a week."

"About a week! Whoa, wait a minute." As Ben Stelson waved his hand, the chimp grabbed one of his fingers and put it in his mouth.

"I think he's hungry, Daddy," Rachel said, moving closer for a better look, Jared and Wetspot right behind her.

"Bright young miss you've got there." Bucky Greene patted her head. It reminded Rachel of the women who patted Wetspot and said, "Cute-looking dog you've got there," when her father took him out for walks. Aside from having the patience of a saint, Ben Stelson was a handsome, not-quite-forty-year-old widower and, as Aunt Lisa put it, "a catch." She'd told Rachel that those women who patted Wetspot "had designs" on her father.

Bucky Greene apparently had designs of his own on her father, but his involved baby-sitting a chimpanzee. Rachel found Bucky's designs a lot more appealing. There were a lot of things Rachel wanted, but a stepmother wasn't one of them. Mickey Phelps, whose real mother lived in California, had one. She was a child psychiatrist. Mickey said she drove him nuts.

Rachel's friend Brianne said the same about hers. Her parents had both remarried, so she had a stepmother *and* a stepfather. She also had a stepbrother from her stepfather, and a stepsister and stepbrother from her stepmother. Other than that, she was an only child.

Fumbling in the pockets of his huge overcoat, Bucky

My Chimp Friday 　　　 9

Greene pulled out a baby bottle. "Here. Give him this. He can drink from a cup, but this is neater when he's moving around. It's plain milk. He likes chocolate milk better—who doesn't?—but save that for a treat. He eats three meals a day. Lettuce, raisins, bread . . . and, of course, bananas."

At that, the chimp gave an interested "hoo-hoo."

"I guess he really likes bananas," Rachel said, and there was a louder "hoo-hoo."

"Believe me, bananas are a very important part of his life," Bucky told her, adding quietly, "and mine, too."

"Say, that's right," Ben said. "Now I remember. You've been working on genetically engineered—"

Bucky thrust his palm in front of Ben's face. "Shhhh."

"Shhhh?"

Bucky nodded. "Trust me. Shhhh."

Jared tugged Rachel's arm and whispered, "He's one to say 'shhhh' after the racket he made."

Rachel told her brother to "shhhh."

Bucky's face grew dark, his voice serious. "I have to leave tonight."

"Where are you going?" Ben asked, equally serious.

"I can't tell you. It's confidential." He lowered his voice again. "And if anyone asks about me, say that you haven't any idea where I went."

"Considering that you're not telling me, that shouldn't be difficult."

"Also, you must not—under any circumstances—let anyone know this chimp is here. His presence has to be kept a secret. I'll explain everything when I return."

"Could you—maybe—explain a little bit now?"

"There's no time." There was definite urgency in Bucky's voice.

"Okay, let me get this straight," Ben said. "You're not going to tell me where you're going. You're not going to tell me why you're going. You're not going to tell me why you're leaving a chimp here. And you're not going to tell me why we can't let anyone know that the chimp is here."

"Correct."

"Well, that certainly clears it all up." Rachel's father smiled.

Bucky Greene didn't smile back. "The less you know, the better."

If that's the case, Rachel thought, it doesn't get much better than this.

"I haven't a lot of time left," he said quickly. "I have to get going."

"Now, Bucky, this is—"

Rachel watched the chimp's tiny hand try to grab the bottle that kept moving out of his reach as her father gestured.

"Daddy, the little guy is *really* hungry. Let me feed him."

"Well, okay." He handed her the bottle.

As she took it, the chimp reached over, threw his arms around her neck, and was suddenly out of her father's grasp and in her arms. For a moment she didn't know who was holding whom, but somehow it didn't matter. It felt really good in a way nothing she could remember had felt in a long time.

She wondered if she might still be dreaming, but not for long. The chimp tightened his grip on her neck.

"Hey, quit the hammerlock. I'm not going to drop you!"

The chimp looked up and blinked, almost as if he understood. But he didn't loosen his grip.

Rachel didn't care. He was the most amazingly adorable creature she had ever seen, let alone held. Dark chocolate eyes were set in a light mocha face that was as soft as the softest suede she had ever touched, and on his chin was a powder-white fuzz of a beard. His hair was silky and black and parted in the center of his head, bristling out at the sides around two comically big ears. It was hard to believe he was real. It crossed her mind that maybe Bucky Greene had created some sort of high-tech, battery-operated toy—which would explain it being "top secret." But the thought disappeared when the chimp pressed his lips against her earlobe. Battery-operated toys—top secret or not—didn't kiss earlobes.

It tickled. Rachel stifled a giggle.

Mickey Phelps had told her she sounded like a mouse with hiccups when she giggled. He'd even tape-recorded her to prove it. She wasn't convinced the recording had proved any similarity between her giggle and a hiccuping mouse—never having heard a mouse hiccup (if in fact mice could hiccup at all)—but thereafter she had tried to avoid giggling whenever she could. It wasn't easy, either. She happened to be extremely ticklish. Her father's nickname for her was Gigglepuss.

"He's more interested in you than in the bottle," Bucky Greene said. "That's good. Here"—he reached into another pocket of his huge coat and handed Rachel a half-eaten banana—"give him this instead."

Rachel took it from him, hoping he wouldn't notice her shiver of distaste as she did. An unwrapped, half-eaten banana. Yuck! She hoped it was the chimp who had eaten the first half. What else did Bucky Greene keep in that coat? And did she really want to know?

Hester Mundis

"Give it to him already," Jared said.

"I will, I will," Rachel said. She certainly wasn't saving it for herself.

Holding the fruit up over her shoulder so that the chimp could see it, she said, "Want a nana?"

"Nana!" Bucky Greene's face suddenly turned white. "Why did you say 'nana'?"

"Well, excuse me," Rachel said, more tartly than she intended. What was his problem? She held up the fruit again, this time enunciating clearly. "Want a *BAnana?*"

The chimp's answer was a machine-gun series of excited "uh-uh-uh-uhs."

"I'll take that as a *yes*," Rachel said. Almost before the words were out of her mouth, the fruit was sucked from her fingers.

"Cool," Jared said.

Bucky Greene let out a relieved breath. "There, you see. Nothing to it. He's happy here already."

"Now, just a minute, Bucky . . . ," Rachel's father began.

"It's only for a week," Bucky called over his shoulder as he dashed for the elevator.

"You can't do this to me, Bucky," Rachel's father pleaded. "I have a job, the kids have school. I'm a biologist, not a zoologist. And—"

"And," Rachel shouted, "you didn't even tell us his name!"

"See you, Friday!" Bucky Greene waved as the elevator door slid closed.

And then he was gone.

"So, is that his name?" Rachel asked as her father shut the door.

"Is what whose name?" Ben Stelson looked a little

My Chimp Friday

dazed and totally baffled. He looked as if he'd just read in one of his journals that new studies had proved that the moon really was made of green cheese.

"The chimp's name. Your friend called him 'Friday.'"

"My *friend*," Ben Stelson explained, emphasizing the word in a way that made it clear that at that moment Bucky was anything but, "said, 'See you, Friday,' meaning that he won't be back for a week! And of all fifty-two of them he could have picked to not be back for, this is the worst."

It might not have been the worst, but it was pretty bad at best.

This was the one week that Rachel's father had midterm exams to grade as well as one-on-one student conferences (which Rachel knew from past experience always strained his "saintly patience"). And he had already agreed to do something that she knew he didn't want to do. He'd promised Aunt Lisa that he would escort a friend of hers whom he'd never met to a black-tie dinner. And if there were a couple of things her father REALLY didn't like, they were formal dinners and blind dates.

"He could have just been saying good-bye to his chimp, Daddy," Rachel said encouragingly. "You know, 'See you, Friday. So long, Friday.'"

The chimp let out an interested "hoo-hoo."

"There, you see," Jared said happily. "That proves it. His name *is* Friday."

S-p-e-c-i-o-u-s. Rachel spelled silently in her head.

"I would have preferred it if he'd said Monday." Their father sighed. "But I suppose Friday is as good a name as any."

Friday "hoo-hooed" in agreement.

"Right now, though, I think we could all use some sleep. I have a feeling we're going to need it."

"The chimp can stay in my room, in Wetspot's wire travel crate," Rachel said excitedly. "I'll make a little bed in it. There's a latch, so it can be his cage, too." Before her father could refuse, she kissed his cheek and took off down the hall with Friday hanging around her neck, Jared and Wetspot trailing behind in fascinated Pied Piper pursuit.

Later that night, which was already early the next morning, Rachel was awakened by a soft snuffling sound next to her ear. Friday was curled up beside her, nuzzling her neck. It was like having a favorite stuffed toy come to life. Sleepily, she pulled him closer and nuzzled back.

Then she bolted upright!

How the heck had he gotten out of the crate? She was sure that she'd latched it after tucking him in. Then again, she had been "sure" of things before that she wasn't *really* sure of. (Last year she'd been "sure" the Mets were going to win the World Series after taking the first three games, and then look what happened.) She slid back down and hugged the tired chimp. He hugged her back. He probably missed his mother. Rachel knew what that was like, so she pulled him closer.

What could possibly be "top secret" about a baby chimpanzee?

As she tried to go back to sleep, she thought about everything Bucky Greene had told her father and about all the things he had refused to tell him.

She also thought about Bucky Greene's coat, which was

about the ugliest one she'd ever seen. Personally, she wouldn't be caught dead wearing something like that. Little did she know that less than three months later that coat was going to save her life.

3.

The Morning After
the Night Before

Rachel awoke and immediately realized two things—it was Saturday, and Friday had wet the bed.

And then she realized a third thing. Friday had left the scene of the accident.

Her door was still closed, so he was obviously somewhere in the room. Just then she saw her "Save the Planet" sweatshirt inching across the floor.

"Okay, I know you're under there, you leaky little chimp, so you might as well come out now."

The sweatshirt ignored her and continued on its stealthy way.

Rachel laughed. She reached down and flung it aside with a magician's flourish. Friday "hoo-hooed" happily and rolled over on his back, pummeling the air with his legs. Rachel tickled his belly. "I think we're going to have to get you some—"

"Breakfast!" Jared shouted, and charged into the room waving a long cardboard tube with a banana sticking out of the top of it.

Friday screeched and leaped onto Rachel, his arms gripping her neck like a noose.

"Jared!" Rachel scolded as best she could while trying to free herself from Friday's choke hold. "You scared him!"

"With a banana? Boy, and I thought Wetspot was a wuss."

"You're whirling that thing like a light saber." Rachel stroked Friday's bristling hair as well as her neck. "What is it?"

"It's a banana launcher. Watch this." With that, Jared pushed an inner cardboard tube and sent the banana flying toward her.

Rachel's hand shot up and caught it. "Jared!"

Friday looked from Jared to Rachel and back again, almost as if to say, "That's neat." Then he grabbed the banana and began to peel it.

"Wow. It worked," Jared said. He wasn't really surprised. All of his inventions worked—to some degree, anyway. He'd seen at least twice every James Bond movie ever made. His hero was "Q," the gadget-making scientist who always envisioned the worst possible situations for 007, and prepared him for them. Rachel felt that this probably accounted for Jared's also wanting to be prepared for every possible emergency. And for a nine-year-old, her brother imagined an awful lot of emergencies. Some of them were just plain silly, not emergencies at all, like his Breakfast Cereal Warning light, a flashlight bulb on a metal strip that lit up when the box was half empty. Like the world would come to an end if they ran out of Cheerios.

Jared plopped down on Rachel's bed and instantly popped back up. "Yuck, it's wet!"

"Friday sprung a leak."

Hester Mundis

"Oh, great, we're baby-sitting a bed-wetting chimp." He rolled his eyes.

"Like you never did that when you were his age?"

"Depends," Jared said. "What *is* his age?"

Rachel shrugged. "Baby?"

"Baby isn't an age. It's a stage of life."

"All right, Mr. Smarty-pants. You know what I mean." Jared was so literal. If someone told him to "go fly a kite," he probably would. Once, when he was younger, their dad said that Uncle Dennis would probably "chew his ear off" when he came to visit and Jared wore earmuffs the whole time Uncle Dennis was there.

Friday was busily squeezing the fruit out of the banana peel, making "uh-uh, uh-uh" noises, when Wetspot entered the room and announced himself. It wasn't much of a bark, as dog barks go, but it was enough to scare the banana out of Friday's hands and cause another unexpected splash-down.

"Oh, no." Rachel groaned. "Not again."

"Oh, yes," said Jared, "again." He pointed at the rug. "I think we'd better get some paper towels."

Rachel held Friday out in front of her as if he were a dripping bag of groceries. "I think we'd better get some diapers."

Their father, still in pajamas, and barefoot, entered the room. "How's our little night visitor this morning, eh? Getting along with . . . what the—" Ben Stelson lifted his foot and looked down at the rug. Then he looked at Wetspot.

Wetspot looked confused.

"It was Friday, Dad," Rachel explained. "We need diapers."

"I don't know if *we* need them, but he sure does," said Jared.

Just then Wetspot, who was examining the stain, suddenly lifted his leg and reverted to the behavior for which he was named.

"Uh-oh," said Jared.

"Oh, NO!" cried Rachel.

"No! No!" shouted her father, but it was too late. Wetspot looked up as if to say, "Is there a problem?", then wagged his tail.

"I can't believe he did that," Rachel said.

Her father sighed. "It's a bit of hostility, which is understandable, and a bit of his natural instinct to mark over another animal's scent."

"With instincts like that, by the time your friend comes to pick up Friday, it's my room that's going to be in-*stinked!* And just who is that man, anyway?"

"And what did he mean when he said 'top secret'?" asked Jared, the James Bond flavor of the words obviously having heightened his interest.

"Bucky Greene has always had a tendency to be overly dramatic about things, so I wouldn't take that top secret stuff too seriously. I've known him for a long time."

"How long?" asked Rachel. "He's never been here before."

"Bucky's not one for socializing, but we stay in touch. He and I were in college together. Now that I think of it, he was pretty secretive back then, too. He would use code names for places."

"Code names?" Jared's eyes widened.

"Uh-huh. The library was 'the Silenceio,' the cafeteria

was 'the Gas Station'—there were lots of others, but I can't remember them."

"Why did he do that?"

"I think it was so that people who he didn't want knowing his whereabouts wouldn't know where he was. He used to say, 'You never know when you want someone *not* to know something.'"

Rachel and Jared stared blankly at their father.

"Okay. He's always been a bit of a character—well, maybe more than a *bit*—but he has a good heart."

"How come he has a chimpanzee?" Rachel asked.

"He works at Bio-allmeans. It's a privately owned research laboratory in Queens, where they're developing genetically engineered fruits and vegetables. Things like no-spit seedless watermelons, peaches without pits, grapes the size of cantaloupes."

"Frankenfoods," said Rachel disdainfully. She was against anything that might harm any species on the planet, and genetically altered corn had already doomed the monarch butterfly. (It had also done something weird to taco shells, which would have really upset her if she liked Mexican food.)

Her father tapped his chin thoughtfully. "As I recall, Bucky was working on building better bananas. In fact, I seem to remember that he was on the verge of some sort of big banana breakthrough."

"Aunt Lisa told us that bananas were a practically perfect food," said Jared. "How is he going to make them better?"

"Maybe that's the 'top secret' part." Their father grinned.

Friday had finished his banana and was now exploring Rachel's room. It wasn't terribly large as bedrooms go, but there was a lot to explore. Rachel had trouble parting with things. Sometimes she'd pick up some old something, fully intending to throw it away, and then she'd remember where she'd gotten it, how long she'd had it, and why she loved it, and back it would go on the shelf. Silly as it was, she felt responsible for all her *things*. How could she throw out the Chutes and Ladders game she and her mother used to play before bedtime? Or the Nancy Drew mysteries that she read those summers they spent at her grandmother's farm in New Jersey. Or her one-legged monkey doll— Wetspot having mistaken it for a chew toy when he was a puppy. Or her Magic 8 Ball, with its bubble answers—"Yes, Definitely"; "Outlook Not So Good"; "You Can Be Sure of It." (Not that she believed the 8 Ball was really able to foretell the future. But for all the years she'd had it, she was still afraid to ask it a serious question.) Or the Rubik's Cube she used to take with her everywhere. Aside from being addictively challenging, it was her good luck charm. She'd solved the six-sided puzzle three times, although purely by accident. The first time she'd done it, she'd found a ten-dollar bill on the sidewalk. The second time, she'd won the school spelling bee. The third time, her father had surprised her with a new computer. She knew it was foolish to believe that there was any connection between the events and the Cube—but that didn't stop her from hanging on to it for luck.

Friday sniffed Rachel's prized possessions as if whatever scent they had would explain what they were. She'd read that chimpanzees had a slightly better sense of smell than humans, but it was still pretty comical to watch his endlessly curious snuffling, since he had no nose to speak of, just a slight ski-slope curve, and nostrils that were almost flush with his face. Every so often he'd put his lips forward to taste an object before touching it. Rachel couldn't imagine people sniffing and tasting things before touching them. Answering the telephone would be ridiculous—and trying on shoes would be gross!

When Friday picked up her Rubik's Cube, he "hoo-hoo'd" excitedly.

"You like that?" Rachel asked.

Friday bobbed up and down, and then somersaulted to a bowlegged stance with the Cube in his hand.

"Hey, he understood you," Jared exclaimed.

"Sure looks like it," their father said, nodding.

The three of them watched as Friday sat down on the floor and began turning the Cube over in his hands, pointing his index finger at the colored squares.

"Do they see in color?"

"Uh-huh. They're very much like humans."

"Some humans are color blind," Jared pointed out.

"And so are some chimps." Rachel's father smiled in a way that told her he was exhibiting his "saintly patience."

"I read in my *Save the Planet* newsletter that chimpanzees have a really high capacity for learning." Rachel knew quite a bit about animals, particularly endangered species. A dollar of her weekly allowance went to organizations dedicated to saving the environment and its animal inhabitants. The walls of her room were layered with wildlife posters, and her bookshelves were cluttered with ecological newsletters and magazines. Mickey Phelps once estimated that if all the endangered beneficiaries of her weekly allowance were placed end to end, they'd probably go around the world, although he had added that they'd look very silly that way.

"They're very smart animals."

"They've already taught some chimpanzees how to use sign language."

"What's the point of that?" Jared asked.

"Well, after those chimps learned how to sign, they were able to pass it on to others in the group. They became like . . . teachers."

"Monkeys as teachers. That's funny." Jared laughed and twirled his banana launcher.

"They're not monkeys," his father corrected. "They're apes."

"I knew that," Jared said quickly, unsuccessfully attempting to cover the fact that he hadn't known that.

"A lot of people confuse the terms 'apes' and 'monkeys,' as well as the animals themselves, but unlike monkeys, apes have no tails."

Rachel had the feeling her father was going into professorial mode. It could be a long morning. Once her dad started explaining something, he tended to provide more detail than necessary. Usually much more than necessary—and neither Rachel nor her brother had inherited their father's saintly patience.

"The chimpanzee," he explained, "is one of the great apes. The gorilla and the orangutan are others."

"What makes them so *great?*" Jared asked.

"It's a classification, not a personality characteristic. But I do recall that at a university in Ohio they're teaching chimpanzees to communicate using printed words, and that's pretty great."

"Pretty dumb, if you ask me," Jared scoffed. "Who are

they going to write letters to? Now, if they taught them how to grow their own bananas, *that* would be pretty great."

Rachel gave her brother a disdainful look and plopped down beside Friday. "Red," she said as his finger pointed to that square on the Cube. "Can you find another *red* one?"

Friday stared directly into her face, then looked down at the Cube and pointed to another red square.

"Ohmygosh! Did you see that?"

"Get him to do it again!"

"It was a coincidence," their father said calmly.

Rachel turned the Cube in Friday's hand. "Can you find a *red* one again? Find a red one."

Friday held the Cube in one hand and studied it. Then he extended his index finger and pointed.

"Wow! He did it again."

"Ask him to find a yellow one," Jared urged.

"He doesn't know what yellow is."

"Show him."

Rachel placed Friday's finger on a yellow square. "Yellow," she said. "Yellow."

Friday pursed his lips, then put them against the Cube and sniffed.

"He's going to see if he *nose* it," said Jared.

"Very punny." She and her brother would often see who could out-pun the other. It made their father laugh; it drove Aunt Lisa nuts.

"That reminds me, kids," their father began, "I think we should—"

"Daddy, look!" Rachel squealed. Friday's index finger was smack dab in the middle of a yellow square. "He's done it!"

"He did it!" cried Jared.

Friday bobbed excitedly, "hoo-hoo-ed" loudly, and then peed on the rug.

"Uh-oh, now he's *done* it," said Jared.

"I was about to say before that I think we should get him those diapers—and I should have said it before." Her father sighed again. Rachel had to admit he did have saintly patience. Aunt Lisa would have gone ballistic. "I'll get the diapers. You two keep Mr. Faucet there in his crate and see if you can clean up the rug. Your aunt Lisa sees that, and we'll never hear the end of it. The last thing I need right now is to have to deal with your aunt Lisa."

Just then the phone rang.

The last thing her father needed was coming over in an hour.

Hester Mundis

4.

Hide-and-Go-Eeeek!

The imminent arrival of Aunt Lisa put the household into full-scale operation camouflage. That weird little man, Bucky Greene, had been very mysterious, but he had been perfectly clear on one thing: Not *under any circumstances* were they to let anyone know the chimp was there. His presence had to be kept a secret.

Aunt Lisa was no more likely to keep a secret than she was to keep food after its expiration date.

The Stelson apartment was large by New York City standards—three bedrooms, a living room, and a kitchen, and a dining room that was used mostly by Rachel's father as an office. But as comfortably spacious as it was, it wasn't nearly spacious enough for concealing the presence of a real, live chimpanzee.

A chimpanzee who seemed to be very intelligent, very active, and curiously adept at escaping from Wetspot's latched dog crate.

A chimpanzee who, although incapable of human speech, could make thirty-two distinct sounds, more than half of them at noise levels punishable by fines in residential areas. Sounds that ranged, her father had warned them, from grunts, moans, screams, and growls to hoots, barks, whines, and howls. Rachel decided that, if necessary, she'd tell neighbors they were baby-sitting a raucous parrot who used to live in a zoo.

Hiding an ape in their apartment was not going to be easy no matter how you looked at it. And as far as Rachel could see, it looked impossible.

"Aunt Lisa is always poking around. Maybe I can keep her far away from my room if I say I saw a cockroach here this morning." Their aunt's loathing of bugs was as great as her fear of germs. Her idea of a perfect world was one without either. Eliminating them whenever and wherever they were encountered was her personal crusade. She kept a small flyswatter in her purse and used it at the first flutter of tiny wings.

"That might work if we can keep Friday quiet."

As if to say "lots of luck," Friday, who was lying on Rachel's bed as she tried unsuccessfully for the third time to diaper him, made one of his thirty-two distinct sounds. It was an impressively loud locomotive whistle "HOO-HOO!"

"Oh, swell. Listen, you. This is not a game. Aunt Lisa will call in the zoo police if she finds out about you."

"Zoo police?" Jared made a face.

She shot her brother a *shut-up* look. "Come on Friday, stay still!" Able to use his feet as hands, he was pulling off the diaper before Rachel could get it on. No sooner would she be ready to fasten it than he'd kick it open with a triumphant new "hoo-hoo."

"Looks like he *ape-solutely* doesn't want to wear one," said Jared, grinning.

 Hester Mundis

"So it *ape-pears*." Friday had begun playing a game of cat's cradle with her hair. Rachel quickly took advantage of the diversion and pinned his legs with her arm, securing the diaper. "There!" Wiping her hands against each other with satisfaction, she felt as proud as when she'd spelled "disheveled" at the last bee. It was more than coincidence that the word came to mind. Her usually neat, ponytailed brown curly locks were now a complete mess (*d-i-s-h-e-v-e-l-e-d*), but Friday's plumbing was under control.

"Do you think he'll keep it on?"

Rachel crossed her fingers. "*Safari* so good."

Friday bent over and touched his new protective gear, then looked quizzically up at Rachel.

"I like a dry rug, okay? Besides, you look cute in underwear." Rachel gave him a hug, and he wrapped his arms around her neck and hugged her back. It was a long one, and it felt really good. Then suddenly like a kid in a TV commercial who just found out he was going to Disney World, Friday began bouncing up and down on the bed "hoo-hoo-ing" at pretty close to the top of his ape lungs.

Jared shook his head. "Uh-oh. Keeping Friday hidden is going to be REALLY difficult."

At this point, as if to prove the point, Friday broke into a screeching "EEEK, EEEK" that sounded like the noise Rachel's computer made when she logged on to the Internet—only played over a public address system.

"Difficult? Ha! *Hopeless* is more like it." Rachel's shoulders slumped.

Friday scrambled off the bed. Darting across the room, he stopped suddenly in front of Rachel's mirrored closet door. He stared at it, his eyes wide, and pressed his lips tentatively against the glass. Then he moved his hand up and down, watching the chimp in the mirror do the same. Several times he tried to grasp the hand in the mirror, hooting in frustration. When he turned around, he appeared bewildered.

"He probably thinks it's another chimp and wonders why it won't play with him," Jared said.

"I hope not. That would be so sad." Rachel pointed to the mirror and then to Friday. "That's you."

Friday pointed to the mirror and then to himself.

"That's right. That's you!"

He peered behind the closet door, then looked back at the mirror. He pointed to himself.

"You," repeated Rachel. Then she pointed to herself and said, "Me."

Friday scratched his head.

"You're confusing him," Jared said. "He thinks he's the 'you' and you're the 'me.'"

"No, he doesn't," Rachel said defensively, silently fearing that he did. How was someone supposed to explain the concept of "you" and "me" to a baby ape, anyway? To a baby anything, for that matter. It was very confusing. After all, everyone was a "me" and a "you" at different times. And sometimes a "me" was an "I." And besides, what difference could a pronoun possibly make to a chimpanzee?

Looking back, Rachel would realize it could mean the difference between his life and death.

"Aunt Lisa will be here any minute," Jared said. "What are we going to do?"

"The best we can." Rachel opened Wetspot's crate and gently put Friday in and latched it. She hesitated for a moment, then quickly pulled a lace from her sneaker and tied it around the latch.

Hester Mundis

"What's that for?"

"Insurance."

Friday stretched his small arm through the bars toward Rachel and "hoo-ed."

She put her hands on her hips and shook her head. "Make me feel guilty, why don't you."

Friday pointed to himself.

"See," Jared gloated, "he does think he's 'you.'"

"You, me—what difference does it make? He's a chimpanzee." Rachel was rarely short-tempered with her brother except on occasions when she was under pressure—like studying for a test, or late for school, or when Aunt Lisa could discover they had an ape in the house and cause an upheaval that would make the eruption of Mount Saint Helens seem like the "pop" of a Rice Krispie.

Friday's arm reached through the bars again. He was pointing to the bottom shelf of Rachel's bookcase.

"You want this?" Rachel held out the Rubik's Cube.

Friday nodded.

"Well, okay. Maybe it will keep you quiet."

For a moment, while he sat on the floor of the crate examining the Cube, it did. Then the buzzer rang, and he let out a shriek to match it.

"Turn on the TV. Quick." Rachel threw her bathrobe over the crate. "And turn it up. Loud."

The buzzer blared again. Friday let out another shriek.

Wetspot, joining the escalating clamor, added a few competitive "woofs" from the hall—which in turn brought another round of hoots from Friday. Determined to get the last bark, Wetspot "woofed" again, restarting the cycle and triggering barks from his pal Attila three stories below that echoed in the courtyard.

My Chimp Friday

"Oh, no." Rachel groaned. At this rate of accelerating noise, even a parrot-who-lived-in-a-zoo story would be questioned.

Jared flipped quickly through channels. "I think we're in luck," he said.

"We're in something, for sure."

"There's a *Tarzan* movie on."

"So?"

Just then Tarzan's chimp, Cheetah, blasted one of her own thirty-two distinct sounds. And it was a humdinger!

Rachel pulled her arm down like Casey Jones mounting to the cabin. "Yes!" She blew a kiss to the screen. "Thank you, Cheetah!" It was the ideal cover. She hoped.

Aunt Lisa's high-pitched voice was calling "hello" from the hall. She drew the word out so it sounded like "hel-loo." It was more like the loon's mating call Rachel had heard when they were in Maine than a greeting. Then again, Aunt Lisa was a bit of a loon.

"Let me look at you." Rachel's aunt stepped back after hugging her. "Hmm. I see we have decided to pass on hair-brushing for the weekend, eh?" She poked at Rachel's disheveled hair with two fingers as if it were something she didn't want to eat.

"We were playing," Jared said. "I mussed it up."

Rachel winked at her brother. She owed him a game of Battleship.

Rachel's father was holding a suit covered in a zippered plastic bag. "Really, Lisa, you shouldn't have gone out of your way to bring this over. I would have picked it up at your place."

"For you, nothing is out of my way."

"But—"

"Forget the 'buts.' It was my pleasure to sew on those buttons." She turned to Rachel. "I wanted to make sure that your dad had his tuxedo—and that he remembered he was taking my friend Mona to that formal dinner tonight."

Rachel rolled her eyes. How could her father forget? Aunt Lisa had called every night that week to remind him. She somehow felt it was her mission to determine who her late sister's husband, "the catch," should and shouldn't date. She'd told Rachel that it was because she didn't want her "favorite" (*only*) niece and nephew winding up with an evil stepmother. She meant well—but it bugged the heck out of all of them.

"Your father has so much to think about, I just want to do my little part to make things easier."

That'll be the day, Rachel thought. Aunt Lisa could complicate making Jell-O.

"I'll be back later to—whoa! What was that?" There was a screech from Rachel's room.

"The television," Rachel and Jared said together.

"And who, may I ask, is watching it?"

"Nobody!" Rachel said quickly.

"Then let me ask you this," Aunt Lisa said patiently. "Do you think your father is a millionaire? That money grows on trees? That you should just leave the television on to keep your furniture company? Hmm?"

It made Rachel want to scream when Aunt Lisa asked dumb questions instead of just saying what she wanted to say, which was: Turn the television off if no one is watching it. "It's a *Tarzan* movie," said Rachel.

My Chimp Friday 33

"I'm going back to see the end of it," said Jared, adding, "I'm not afraid of a *cockroach.*"

Aunt Lisa turned pale. "Cockroach?" Her eyes became huge. "You have cockroaches?"

Rachel owed her brother more than one game of Battleship. "It was a bug. I don't know if it was a roach. I'm sure it's gone." She watched as her aunt began to grimace. "I mean, it was crawling very fast."

Aunt Lisa stiffened. "I'm not going in there."

"It's a good movie," Rachel said innocently. She was clamping hard on a smile. The "Gigglepuss" in her was making headway.

"I have too many errands," she said hurriedly, trying to avoid Wetspot, who'd come forward for a sniff. "Good dog." She petted Wetspot with the same two-fingered push she had used on Rachel's hair.

"He is a good dog, isn't he?" Rachel bent down and kissed him on the nose.

"Oooooh!" The look on Aunt Lisa's face was worth the reprimand Rachel knew was coming. "Have you any idea where that dog's nose has been?"

Actually, Rachel had a pretty good idea of where his nose had been. But her aunt would probably faint if she ever got the specifics. Rachel didn't really like to think of them herself.

"Wash your face and brush your teeth immediately. Oooh." She shivered. "I'll be back this evening around six." She leaned forward to kiss Rachel but then changed it to an awkward pat on the shoulder.

"You really don't have to, Aunt Lisa. I can make dinner for us."

"You're growing kids. You need healthy food, lots of veggies. Besides, I have a new recipe. You'll love it."

Rachel seriously doubted that she'd love it. And when her aunt confided that her new recipe was for a tuna-tofu tomato surprise, all doubt was replaced with certainty. Yuck city!

As Aunt Lisa was saying good-bye, a loud series of rapid-fire hoots blared from the bedroom.

Rachel held her breath.

"For heaven's sake, turn that television down. It sounds like a zoo in here."

Rachel nodded and was barely able to contain her laughter as she closed the door.

"All clear?" Jared asked.

"All clear." Giggling, she hurried back to her bedroom and pulled the bathrobe off the crate. What she saw was as amazing as it was unexplainable. Friday was sitting cross-legged and happily examining the sides of the Rubik's Cube he'd been playing with. Only now each side was a solid color!

"Jared, look! He's solved the puzzle! The chances of that happening must be a bazillion gazillion to one!"

"There's no such number as a bazillion gazillion."

Rachel gave her brother a tired look. She picked Friday up and nuzzled him. "You, little guy, have no idea what you just did. And I'll bet no one in the world would believe that you did it."

The odds were a bazillion gazillion to one, but she was wrong on both counts.

5.

King of the Jumble

Couldn't I just ask Peter to come over?" Jared pleaded. "He'd be so impressed."

"He's the world's biggest snoop and blabbermouth. Forget it," Rachel said. It had been hard enough keeping Aunt Lisa in the dark for the past six days—and *she* wasn't curious about anything that didn't directly involve her and germs, or their father's love life.

The night she'd made her tuna-tofu tomato surprise for them, Rachel had dressed Friday in her Raggedy Ann doll's clothes, put the doll's red wig on him, and carried him through the living room. Twice. All Aunt Lisa said was, "Don't you think you're too old to still be playing with dolls?"

Rachel had wanted to scream something nasty, but she hadn't. Aunt Lisa was constantly telling her that she was either too old or too young for things. Too old for dolls, too young for dates; too old for cartoons, too young for soap operas; too old for balloons, too young for blush. Grrrr. It made no sense to have to outgrow things that you enjoyed and grow into things that you wanted to.

It also made no sense trying to argue with Aunt Lisa. Fortunately, she was only concerned with what concerned her—which worked out swell as far as concealing Friday was concerned.

She hadn't even noticed the rope pulleys in Rachel's bedroom. Jared had devised a system using clothesline and a cardboard carton that could hoist the box and whisk Friday into hiding. He called it the Upmobile. Friday thought it was a ride and loved it. Aunt Lisa thought it was just another of Jared's Rube Goldberg inventions and didn't question it. (Asking Jared about his inventions usually let you in for more than you needed to know or had time to listen to.)

"Boy." Jared dug the toe of his sneaker into the carpet. "We have a chimpanzee in our apartment. Probably the most exciting thing that's ever happened to us. And we can't tell anyone about it. That stinks."

It really did. Their housekeeper, Mrs. Carey, was the only other person who knew about Friday, but she just accepted his presence, and keeping it secret, as normal. Mrs. Carey used to work in crowd control at the Macy's Thanksgiving Day Parade and was hard to fluster. Mickey and Brianne, on the other hand, would flip if they knew about Friday. Like Rachel, they were also members of *Save the Planet*. In fact, this year for the school's Earth Day competition, the three of them were preparing an exhibit about Africa's endangered natural habitats—especially those for apes. They would go bananas for the chance to play with a real chimpanzee. Then again, who wouldn't?

Well, maybe not snooty Karla Nesmith. She didn't like to do anything that most other kids in their class did—mostly because she felt they were not in her class.

My Chimp Friday

Stuck-up, conceited, rich, and spoiled, Karla's only friends were kids who were impressed by her wealth. Rachel had tried being friendly on several occasions, but Karla wasn't interested. Karla wasn't interested in anything but herself.

Unfortunately—and unfairly—she was also the prettiest girl in their school.

Friday was in the Upmobile holding on to the clothesline with one hand and a half of a banana with the other when Rachel's father came in and announced he'd gotten an e-mail from Bucky Greene.

"What does it say?" Rachel craned her neck to see the screen of her father's laptop computer.

The message was in all capital letters. "'SUBJECT: TOP SECRET,'" Rachel read aloud. "How corny can you get?

"'I AM BACK IN THE COUNTRY, BUT I CAN'T COME TO THE CITY. YOU MUST CONTINUE TO KEEP MERGATROID'S PRESENCE IN YOUR APARTMENT A SECRET!'

"Mergatroid!" Rachel cried. "I think he should have kept that name a secret. *Mergatroid!"*

Friday hooted and tugged excitedly on the pulleys.

Rachel looked up. "As long as you're with us, you're Friday, okay . . . Mergatroid?"

Friday hooted again.

"I'm not calling him that name," she mumbled.

"What else does it say?" Jared asked.

"'UNDER NO CIRCUMSTANCES SHOULD YOU BRING HIM BACK TO THE BIO-ALLMEANS LAB.

THERE ARE REASONS. REASONS I CAN'T EXPLAIN NOW BUT I WILL EXPLAIN WHEN I CAN. BEE GEE.'"

"That's it?"

"That's it."

"But he doesn't say when he's coming or where he is."

"That's Bucky for you," her father said. "Don't worry. He'll turn up soon."

And sure enough he did. He turned up the very next day in the newspaper.

Dead.

6.

Bad Bunch

The newspaper said that Bucky Greene had been found dead at his upstate New York home. According to the report, he had just returned that day from a trip to Kenya, apparently had slipped on a banana peel, and had fallen into an empty concrete swimming pool.

The headline read: DNA SCIENTIST D.O.A.

There was a picture of a smiling Bucky Greene beneath it. He wasn't wearing that horrible monstrosity of a coat, which was probably why he was smiling.

Rachel reread the article and shook her head. "How ironic." It was another of Mr. DeFina's enriching words, but it certainly fit the situation. Her father had told her that one of Bucky's genetically modified bananas had a nonslip peel.

"It's very sad." Her father sighed. "He was a good man and a fine scientist."

"Don't you think this could be more than just an accident?" Rachel asked earnestly. "I mean, especially since he told us that keeping Friday hidden here was *top secret?*"

"Bucky liked being dramatic. A minor discovery for

another scientist would be a world-shattering break-through for Buck. Nope. I'm afraid that what happened was just an unfortunate coincidence where a banana peel was in the wrong place at the wrong time."

Rachel had her doubts, but she decided to keep them to herself. Her father would probably say that she was being overly suspicious, which she did have a tendency to be ever since she gotten hooked on reading Nancy Drew mysteries. But she'd be willing to bet her Rubik's Cube that Bucky Greene had not just "slipped away."

Friday pointed to the picture of Bucky and seemed perplexed.

"I think he recognizes him!" Rachel spread the newspaper on the floor.

Friday traced Bucky's smiling face with his finger. Then he bent down and pressed his lips against it.

The sudden sharp ache in Rachel's chest took her by surprise. It was familiar, but it was so unexpected and so great that she felt as if someone had punched her. Bucky was probably the only parent Friday had ever known and now he was gone forever. He was never coming back. She understood that loss even if Friday didn't, and somehow it pained her all the more because of it.

Rachel scooped Friday into her arms and held him tightly. He leaned over and looked down at the picture again. "I'm sorry," she murmured. She really was.

Her father ruffled her hair and kissed her head. Somehow he always knew when she needed that. She was glad he did.

"We're going to keep him, aren't we, Daddy? I mean, he's all alone now. Just look at him. He's so sad."

As if he understood, Friday made the softest, most

pathetic little whimper. It was from someplace other than his roster of thirty-two distinct sounds.

"Well . . . he doesn't really belong to us."

"Sure, he does. Bucky gave him to us. But now Bucky is . . . dead, and we're not, so Friday is ours." Rachel found herself spelling s-p-e-c-i-o-u-s in her head. That word was really getting to bug her.

"Besides," Jared said, "didn't Bucky say we shouldn't return him to that lab?"

"Yes, but he was . . . alive then."

"Then what he told us was a dying man's wish," Rachel said excitedly. "And you know what they say about a dying man's wish."

"That it's his last?"

"Daddy!"

"Look, honey, an ape is a wild animal. He's not meant to be a pet. We don't have to return him to the lab. We can send him to a nice zoo."

"ZOO?"

Friday shrieked and leaped from Rachel's arms. Grabbing the ropes of the Upmobile, he climbed to the top of her bookcase and crouched down, shaking his head.

"See. He doesn't want to go to a zoo," Rachel said.

"He doesn't know what a zoo is, honey."

Friday stood and stamped his feet, swaying from side to side as he continued to shake his head.

"He sure looks as if he knows. And he sure doesn't want to go."

"How would he know what a zoo is? He's been raised in a laboratory."

"Maybe one of the other chimps at the lab came from a zoo," Rachel offered. "Or he could have seen something on television. There was probably one at the lab because he knows how to turn ours on."

"Really?" Her father looked surprised.

"Really." Rachel called, "Hey you!" Friday pointed to himself. "That's right, you. Want to come down and watch some TV?"

Friday held the rope in one hand and slid down as smoothly as melting ice cream. Bounding across the room, he flipped the television's ON switch and plopped down in front of it.

"He likes to watch the Discovery Channel. Especially when there's something about chimps."

"Otherwise it's mostly MTV," Jared said. "He goes for those music videos."

Their father stared. "That's remarkable."

"Yeah. He's pretty smart." Friday reached for the remote control, but Rachel whisked it away. "Oh, no, you don't. I showed him the channel changing button the other day, and he's worse than Jared." Her brother flipped through channels at warp speed.

"He can even do a few things on the computer. I showed him how to point the cursor to bring up my animal pictures. He loves the ones of chimps. Watch." She stood him in front of her computer. "Go ahead, find the pictures."

Friday leaned forward, moving the mouse with his right hand. When the arrow pointed to a camera icon, he clicked it and a photograph of a group of chimpanzees grooming one another in the jungle unfolded on the monitor.

"There. What did I tell you?"

"That's . . . that's extraordinary." Her father was really

impressed, which made Rachel feel terrific. Things that would make other kids' dads' jaws drop were taken in stride by hers. Being a professor, Rachel's father believed that everything—with the possible exception of Aunt Lisa's compulsive matchmaking—had a perfectly rational explanation.

Friday ran his index finger slowly over the image of a small chimp who was sitting off to the side. It was what he'd done with the photo of Bucky Greene. Rachel wondered if the chimp on the computer screen reminded him of someone, too.

"If you think that's something, watch this." Jared nudged Friday to the side and sat himself in front of the computer. The game of solitaire appeared. "Okay, Friday, let's play."

Friday climbed into Jared's lap. When each new card came up, he'd point to where he wanted it moved, then give a satisfied little hoot.

"He watched me play the other day and he, well, just sort of got it. But he hasn't figured out what to do with the aces yet." Jared tapped him on the head. "Have *you?*"

Friday pointed to himself and shook his head.

"Pretty impressive, huh? So can we keep him?"

Her father ran his fingers abstractedly through his hair. "Chimpanzees are intelligent, but . . . but Friday is doing things that should take years for him to learn."

"So was Jared when he was little," Rachel reminded him. Her brother had amazed everyone on his fourth birthday by constructing a three-room intercom by using batteries and bits from broken toys. "Friday's a smart chimp—which is all the more reason for us to keep him."

"Can we, Dad?"

"Please?"

"Well . . . ," her father drawled, "I don't know." It was a good sign. Whenever their father answered indefinitely, it usually turned out to be a "yes."

"Bucky was your friend. You know he must have had a good reason for leaving . . . Friday"—she'd be darned if she would call him Mergatroid—"with us."

"I only wish I knew the reason."

"But you do," Rachel said brightly

"I do?"

"Sure you do. He told you."

"What was it?"

She grinned. "Top secret!"

Her father smiled tiredly. "Okay. Okay. This is probably the craziest thing I've ever agreed to. I just hope we're doing the right thing."

"Of course we are," Rachel said, nodding toward Friday, who was once again playing with the computer. "Look how much fun he's having with us here."

"But is *here* where he belongs?" Her father cocked his head toward the computer screen, where Friday was again touching the pictures of the chimpanzees. "It's something to think about, you know."

Rachel knew. But she certainly wasn't going to think about it.

7.

Keeping Eyes and
Bananas Peeled

The Dahl School lunchroom was noisier than usual when Rachel made her way to the table where Brianne and Mickey were waiting for her.

"So can you finally tell us your *big* secret?" Brianne asked, chewing on a celery stick and sounding as if she couldn't care less, which couldn't have been further from the truth. She was Rachel's best friend, and had been since kindergarten when the two of them had bonded over identical pink angora sweaters and would pretend that they were sisters, but boy was she nosy. If something was none of her business, she wanted to know what it was and why it wasn't her business. Mickey and Rachel long ago had decided that it was some sort of ego thing for her, like wanting to be "the girl most informed about matters not concerning herself," so neither held it against her. They certainly couldn't hold it over her; Brianne was taller than both of them. In fact, she was the tallest girl in the school.

Interestingly, with all the things that Brianne did know, she rarely, if ever, gossiped, which was a good thing.

It was one of the reasons that she and Rachel had remained best friends. When Rachel's mother was in the hospital, and Rachel had felt more alone than she could imagine anyone possibly feeling, Brianne was there every day to confide in, and to cry with. Over the years they'd known each other, Rachel had told Brianne a lot that she sometimes wished she hadn't. But it didn't matter. That's what best friends are for. And, although far from perfect, Brianne was always there for her.

Mickey Phelps was also a best friend. Despite his practical joking, and their being competitive in everything from spelling bees to solving puzzles, Rachel genuinely enjoyed his company. He was intelligent and funny and was always willing to listen to what she had to say. Not that he always agreed with her, but that wasn't important.

Rachel had planned on telling them about Friday when Bucky returned. But now that Bucky wasn't ever returning and Friday was part of the family, Rachel couldn't think of any reason why she still had to keep him a secret.

"Go," Mickey said when she sat down. "You've been Ms. Mystery all week."

"Well, let me put it this way." Rachel paused and bit her lower lip thoughtfully, her eyes twinkling. "I think I'd rather *show* than tell."

"Okay," said Brianne, "then on with the *show*."

"You'll have to come back to my house with me after school."

"How come?"

"You'll see."

"See what?"

"I said, you'll *see!*"

Brianne sighed. "This better be good."

My Chimp Friday

"This," said Rachel, grinning, "is way better than good!"

As they entered the black-and-white-tiled lobby of her apartment building, Rachel noticed that the attractive dark-haired woman she'd seen hanging around the entrance for the past three days studying the names on the buzzers was now inside the lobby looking at the mailboxes. She made a mental note to mention it to Mr. Aplox, the superintendent. When the Wallersteins, who lived in 2J, went to Florida last month, their apartment was burglarized. The thieves took their stereo, Mr. Wallerstein's computers, and a Picasso print that she'd heard was worth more than the stereo and computers combined. Just because the stranger was a woman didn't mean she couldn't be a burglar—or an accomplice to one.

Now that she thought about it, there had been an odd, square-headed guy with a funny little pickle nose—it looked like a gherkin—hanging around across the street recently. He wore dark sunglasses all the time—even the other day, when it was really overcast. Unfortunately, it hadn't been overcast enough to keep her from seeing him repeatedly wipe his pickle nose on his jacket. It was gross. Nonetheless, for all anyone knew, the two of them—the attractive dark-haired lady and sleeve-wiping pickle nose—could be in cahoots.

"You are reading way too many mysteries," Mickey said when she told them this in the elevator.

"You can say that again," Brianne muttered.

"What's that supposed to mean?"

"What's it mean? It means that when Karla Nesmith refused to have the Math Club at her house, you suspected it was because she had something hidden there—like a body."

"You know I didn't mean that. I just don't understand someone being so unfriendly to everyone in school for no reason."

"There is a reason. She's not a nice person. Face it, Rachel, there are nice people and there are not-nice people. Karla's not a nice person. Her family is really, really rich, she's really, really spoiled, and she believes we aren't 'la-di-da' enough for her fancy world." Brianne put her nose in the air and sniffed haughtily. Then she sneezed twice.

"*Gesundheit!*" said Rachel.

"Whatever." Brianne dabbed her nose with a tissue.

Outside the apartment door, Rachel stopped and held up her palm. "Listen, I don't want everyone to know about this. So I want you both to promise that you'll keep my secret a secret."

"Now we have to keep your secret a secret? This is"—Brianne sneezed again—"getting a little ridiculous."

"Promise?"

"Promise," Brianne said reluctantly.

"What do you have in there? The missing link?"

"You'll see." Rachel opened the door. Wetspot trotted toward them, tail wagging. He knew Mickey was always good for a long scratch behind the ears.

"Yo, Wetspot! Are you guarding the *secret?*" Mickey laughed and hummed the opening to *The Twilight Zone*.

Brianne double-sneezed again.

Whether it was Brianne's sneezes, Mickey's laugh, or *The Twilight Zone* de-de-de-des that did it, Rachel would never know. But suddenly Friday dropped out of nowhere (from atop the hall bookcase, actually), screeching one of his shrill thirty-two distinct sounds (Jared had dubbed this particular one "the ambulance"), in a fur-bristling, chest-thumping entrance worthy of King Kong with a hotfoot.

Brianne threw her arms up in reflexive defense, her books tumbling to the floor, and shrieked almost as loud as Friday. "Ohmygod! It's . . . it's . . ."

"A chimpanzee," said Rachel.

"Well, I'll be a monkey's uncle," Mickey breathed.

Rachel rolled her eyes, smoothing Friday's bristled fur as she lifted him. "It's all right, Friday. These are my friends."

Friday "hooted" softly. It was pure magic.

Not in Rachel's wildest wishes for this moment had she imagined the delicious impact Friday would have on her friends. She used to wonder what being "ga-ga" over something actually looked like. Now she knew. Mickey's and Brianne's eyes were saucer-wide, and their mouths were open as if they'd been frozen. They were definitely ga-ga over Friday.

"He is too adorable for words," Brianne gushed. She was well over her initial surprise, which Rachel suspected of being over the top, anyway. Cocking her head from side to side, she repeated "hello" several times, as if she were talking to a parrot. Then, switching to, "How do you do?" she extended her hand and shook Friday's. He looked confused, but went along with it. He was obviously getting the hang of humoring humans.

"Can I hold him? Oh, please?" Brianne held out her arms, and Rachel placed Friday in them. "You are sooo cute," she cooed, adding "ooochy, mooochy, scooochy" baby talk sounds as if he'd understand those better.

"Don't hog him, Brianne," Mickey said, reaching

around to shake Friday's hand, too. "Let me have him for a while."

"So," said Rachel, "was I right in wanting to show rather than tell?"

Neither Brianne nor Mickey answered. They were too engrossed in Friday, who was delighted with the attention he was getting. Who wasn't delighted with the attention Friday was getting was Wetspot. He made this perfectly clear with a very decisive lift of his leg.

Rachel squealed, "No!" but was too late.

Brianne's books were a washout.

Jared raced out of his room. "Uh-oh. Looks like we've got trouble right here in River City."

River City was right. If Wetspot continued at this rate, the apartment would become Atlantis! Rachel felt responsible, so she spent the next hour with Jared making new covers for Brianne's books from brown paper bags while Brianne and Mickey played a game of catch the grape with Friday, who—unlike Wetspot—was quite adept at retrieving everything. Grapes were a favorite.

Wetspot was confined to quarters for the remainder of the afternoon; "quarters" being his old crate, the one that had become Friday's bedroom, which sort of added insult to injury. Rachel felt bad about that, but he couldn't continue to demonstrate his hostility so . . . so . . . demonstrably. Jealousy was understandable, but it didn't have to stain carpets.

Before they left, Rachel decided to tell Mickey and Brianne her suspicions about what really had happened to Bucky. She showed them the article in the newspaper.

"I know you think I read too many mysteries and get suspicious too often, but doesn't what I've told you sound a little . . . suspicious? A top-banana banana scientist slips on a no-skid banana peel after asking us to hide a top secret chimp?"

Brianne shrugged. No one could accuse her of having an overactive imagination.

Mickey sucked his cheek thoughtfully. "Could be. Are the police investigating?"

"Well . . . they don't know about Friday or about Bucky saying we had to keep him a secret."

"Maybe you should tell them."

"I guess. But then they might take Friday away, hold him as evidence. Or worse. Take him back to the laboratory." All of a sudden, Rachel wished she had kept her suspicions to herself. "I'm a goose. I don't know why I even mentioned it." She laughed. "Come on. Let me show you the Upmobile."

Later that evening, when her father returned home, Rachel thought about telling him her suspicions, but changed her mind. He had been reluctant about letting them keep a chimpanzee in the first place. If Friday were needed for an investigation, they'd have to give him up. Besides, it was probably just her inner sleuth overreacting again. She couldn't walk five blocks without noticing a dozen suspicious things.

There was probably, she assured herself—as her father often said—a perfectly reasonable and not necessarily scary explanation for everything. Everything, that is, except Aunt Lisa's never-ending attempts to find a match for "the catch." Rachel shuddered. She hated when her aunt referred to her father as "the catch." It made him sound like a dead fish. Aunt Lisa had confided to her earlier on the phone in one of their weekly "let's talk girl talk bonding calls" (which were as much fun for Rachel as getting a paper cut) that she'd told a new friend of hers all about her brother-in-law, "the catch."

"So I said to Wendy, that's her name, Wendy—you know, like Wendy in *Peter Pan?*—only her name is Wendy Mills. Nice name, isn't it?"

Like her name mattered? "Very nice."

"I said that aside from having the patience of a saint, your father looked like a cross between Mel Gibson and Tom Cruise. And I suggested"—she had lowered her voice to a gleeful whisper—"that she surreptitiously, you know, sneakily, check him out."

"Why didn't you just show her his picture?"

"It's not the same thing. Besides, I thought maybe she could, you know, accidentally run into him. Just happen to be coming around the corner or waiting for someone near the building. Something he wouldn't think was a setup."

Her father would never think it was a setup because he would never think someone would set up anything so dumb. As much as he was aware of Aunt Lisa's matchmaking mania, he underestimated it. This time she had sent him a stalker. A sneaky female stalker! It was creepy. It could even be against the law. But at least it explained who the dark-haired woman hanging around their lobby was and why she was there.

What it didn't explain, though, was the presence across the street of that pickle-nosed guy with the sunglasses. Then again, it didn't explain why birds sleep standing up, either. Rachel decided to forget about both.

8.

Catching Trouble

"**I** think he's coming down with something," Mrs. Carey said when Rachel returned from school the following day. She was rocking Friday in her arms. His tan face was flushed, and his nose was running.

Rachel put down her schoolbooks and felt his forehead. It was really warm. "Oh, no. What's wrong?"

Friday looked as if he were thinking about it. Then he sneezed twice.

"He's caught Brianne's cold." Rachel smacked the side of her head. "I totally forgot that chimpanzees can catch people diseases. And there I was happily watching as she was shaking his hand and sneezing on him. It's all my fault."

Friday sneezed twice again. Rachel remembered reading that double sneezes boded double trouble. Fortunately, it was just a ridiculous superstition. Unfortunately, she was ridiculously superstitious.

"No point in blaming anyone." Mrs. Carey handed Friday to Rachel. "I'll make some herbal tea and find nose drops. You get him into something warm. And if he's going to be walking around, he needs to have something on his legs and feet."

"Like pajamas—or what?"

"Anything that will keep him evenly covered."

Some things are easier said than done, and evenly covering a chimpanzee, Rachel discovered, was one of them.

"He can wear my old woolen T-shirt," Jared offered.

"Okay. Get it." Rachel rummaged through the drawers of her bureau. "And think of something we can use for pants."

Jared put the T-shirt over Friday's head; it hung down to his toes. He looked like he had shrunk in the wash.

"That covers his legs," said Jared, but almost before the words were out, so were Friday's legs. He somersaulted onto Rachel's bed and began kicking his feet in the air. For a sick chimp he seemed well into having a good time.

In one last desperate attempt, Rachel grabbed a pair of her long woolen socks and tried to keep them on his legs with rubber bands. He looked like a rubber-banded, bandy-legged war prisoner and definitely not happy about it; he had the socks off in seconds.

"He'll never stay put under a blanket."

"What if we turned the blanket into bunting? You know, put him in it and tie it around his waist. It's worth a try."

It was worth a try. But just for laughs. Friday reacted as if he were in a potato sack race. Pushing off easily on his knuckles, he made very good time, too.

Mrs. Carey picked him up and laid him in her lap. "Here now. Let me just give him some nose drops."

Once again this was something easier said than done.

The moment Friday spied the dropper approaching, he

turned his head in the other direction. If it was coming from the left, his face was going to the right.

"This will make you feel better," Mrs. Carey cooed as she attempted to zero in on his nose. But Friday wasn't lying still for that. He wasn't lying still, period. In desperation, Mrs. Carey squeezed a few blind squirts at his nostrils, but the drops only dripped down his cheeks.

Rachel and Jared tried not to giggle, but it was funny.

When it was clear that Friday was having none of her nose drops, Mrs. Carey brought in a cup of warm tea with honey, which he drank with "uh-uh-uh" appreciation.

"Well, it's probably just a cold," Mrs. Carey said, heartened by Friday's enthusiasm for her tea. "It'll run its course."

But it wasn't "just a cold." The following day, Friday was pale and listless, and his breathing sounded as if he were snoring.

Rachel called her father at work, something she rarely did. He rushed home, took one look at Friday, and within fifteen minutes they were all in a taxi racing across town to the New York Animal Medical Center's emergency room.

The waiting room at the Animal Medical Center was bright and clean and friendlier-looking than most people hospitals Rachel had seen. A young woman with a ferret wrapped in a towel sat in a corner, sniffling softly. Another woman held a small gray dog with a broken leg in her lap. Rachel and Jared sat silently with Friday as their father spoke to a nurse behind the desk.

After a while, a tall, red-haired young man in a white coat came out. He had a warm smile and introduced himself as Dr. Jameson as he brought them into a small examining room.

Friday pulled at the stethoscope with his feet as Dr. Jameson listened to his chest.

Friday was being very good, all things considered. He seemed to know that something was wrong and that he had been brought here to have it fixed.

Dr. Jameson took a deep breath. "What we have here is a very sick chimp."

Rachel's eyes welled with tears. Jared clasped her hand—or maybe it was the other way around—but the grip was tight. Her father put his arm around her shoulder in a way that made the doctor's words seem even more frightening.

"I'm afraid it's a serious respiratory infection. You'll have to leave him here. We'll do everything we can."

Her father nodded.

Friday looked from the doctor to Rachel, then raised his arms toward her to be picked up. Before she could pick him up, though, Dr. Jameson had handed him to a nurse. Rachel barely had enough time to blow a kiss to him before bursting into uncontrollable sobs.

Every afternoon the following week when she returned from school, Rachel phoned the Animal Medical Center to find out how Friday was doing. He had a rare form of pneumonia that Dr. Jameson had never encountered before.

"It's very strange," he told her. "This particular strain has only rarely been found in humans and has never affected apes. Fortunately, though, he is responding well to treatment." He chuckled. "And everyone here is responding well to him. He is a charmer, and extremely bright."

"Yes, I know," Rachel said proudly.

"Quite remarkable, really."

My Chimp Friday

"Really?"

"He amazed everyone here yesterday by unlocking his cage and climbing out."

"He's good at that."

"A regular Houdini. We've had to put a padlock on it to keep him in there."

"How much longer will he have to be there?"

"A few more days. The end of the week is what my assistant told your mother when she called, so I guess I'll—"

"My . . . *mother?*"

"Why, yes. She phoned—"

"You must be mistaken," Rachel said, trying to keep her voice polite. She hoped she didn't have to explain further.

"Really? I'm sure the desk said that Mrs. Stelson called to ask about picking him up. Maybe she didn't want you to know she called. You know, to surprise you."

"Surprise" would be putting it mildly. "My mother is . . . dead." It was always difficult for her to say.

"Oh, I'm terribly sorry. It was probably a name that sounded like Stelson . . . although I could have sworn they told me that the woman was calling about a chimpanzee— and Friday's the only one here. I must have misheard the message. An odd coincidence, though."

Almost as odd a coincidence as a top-banana banana scientist slipping on a no-skid banana peel after hiding a top secret chimp, Rachel thought, her heart suddenly beating rapidly. Maybe her overactive imagination wasn't so overactive after all. And even if it was, she didn't care. She cared about Friday. "Dr. Jameson, you have to promise that you won't release Friday to anyone but me and my father."

"Why, I wouldn't think of—"

Hester Mundis

"I know you wouldn't, but swear that you won't, anyway," Rachel said, unable to disguise the urgency in her voice.

"Is something wrong?"

"I hope not," she said. "I really hope not."

9.

Ripe for the Picking

When they picked Friday up, Dr. Jameson told them again how "way above average" their chimp was. But you couldn't tell that by his behavior on returning home. It was pure chimp. He "hoo-hoo'd," "uh-uh-uh'd," and leaped from couch to chair to tabletop with ape-like abandon.

Rachel and Jared began to sing "If You're Happy and You Know It." Before they got to "clap your hands," Friday was already clapping his. He was definitely happy to be home and showing it.

Wetspot was not as thrilled with the return of the jungle's native son, although he (thankfully) didn't demonstrate it in his previous fashion. Perhaps because of his punishment last time, he decided to forgo the territorial thing and just look forlorn. As Friday cavorted about the apartment, Wetspot lay on the floor, head drooped over his paws, looking about as unhappy a canine camper as you could imagine.

"Daddy, maybe if you take him for a walk in the park it will cheer him up," Rachel suggested. Usually just hearing the words "walk" and "park" would elicit a tornado tail wag from Wetspot. But he doggedly refused to react.

"Come on, fella." Rachel's father shook the leash. Wetspot looked up, expressionless, and then turned his head away.

"Oh, no," Jared moaned. "Now *he's* sick."

"He's not sick, he's sulking." Ben Stelson knelt down and petted their dog. Within a matter of moments, Wetspot's sulk was history. Forlornness forgotten, he was on his back and reflexively thumping his leg in the air, thoroughly enjoying a tummy rub.

Friday climbed down from the table to more closely observe the strange action in progress. Wetspot ignored him. Wetspot ignored almost everything while having his tummy rubbed.

"If Friday could give Wetspot a tummy rub, I'll bet they'd be friends for life," Jared remarked.

"I wonder if he would do it."

As if considering this, Friday placed his hand on top of Rachel's father's, moving it back and forth, learning the motion. Wetspot didn't seem to object. (Nothing came between Wetspot and a tummy rub.) Slowly, their father slipped his hand away and there was Friday giving the tummy rub. It wasn't a "leg thumper," but it was an acceptable doggy tummy rub, and Wetspot was not only accepting it, he was enjoying it—grudgingly, but enjoying it none the less.

"I think they're going to be friends," Rachel said.

"It's a start," her father agreed.

"So the moral of this tale is?"

Jared shrugged.

"The way to a dog's heart is through his tummy."

"Ay," said her father, "and there's the rub."

My Chimp Friday

With Friday's above average intelligence confirmed by Dr. Jameson, Rachel felt more of a responsibility to stimulate it. Boredom, from everything she'd read, was the worst thing for chimps that were not living in the wild. For extra smart chimps not living in the wild, the worst thing had to be even worse. She was determined not to let Friday go from bored to worse.

While she was at school, Rachel left the TV on for him. He already knew how to change the channels, and Mrs. Carey told her that he always switched stations when commercials came on. It kept him occupied and out of trouble. Most of the time.

When there was pizza around, which there often was when Aunt Lisa wasn't, it was another story. Friday was a pizza pirate of prime primate proportions. If Rachel or Jared left a slice unguarded to, say, answer the phone or get a napkin, Friday would take a chimp-sized chunk out of it and then run and hide behind the couch. Sometimes, he'd grab a full slice from the box, Upmobile it to the top of Rachel's bookshelf, and then drop circles of pepperoni (not his favorite topping) to the floor while lying on his back and pulling the cheese off into long strings that he'd suck in like spaghetti.

The main problem with Friday and pizza was his lust for the crust. The outer crispy crusts which Rachel and Jared always left over, were Friday's favorite—not to eat, but to flush down the toilet. To Friday, this was like an arcade game. He'd grab a crust, run to the bathroom and toss it in the bowl, flush it down with a flourish—hooting like crazy as it swirled and disappeared—and then come back for another.

Actually, this wasn't a problem until the night he

decided to deep-six two pies' worth of crusts in a single flush—and the Stelsons' apartment toilet refused to cooperate. With a vengeance. Instead of going down, the water in the bowl and a dozen soggy crusts rose unstoppably back up over the rim and onto the bathroom floor, turning their fuzzy pink bathmat into a squishy, crumb-studded mess that looked like giant animal barf.

Rachel's father tried using a plunger to unclog the crusty overload, but there was a pizza dough buildup in the pipe that wasn't budging. And as if that wasn't bad enough, Friday hopped on the plunger and discovered how to use it as a pogo stick, leaving dark round circles down the hall and on the living room carpet. In the end, Rachel's dad made them hide Friday in Wetspot's crate and called Mr. Aplox. He came with a long wire snake and in about five minutes got everything flowing smoothly again. He didn't ask how all that pizza crust got in the toilet, but he did suggest that it not go there again. Rachel's father was very grateful for his lack of curiosity and gave him a large tip.

Rachel was telling this to Brianne and Mickey when they were at the apartment working on their entry for the Earth Day contest. This year they'd decided on a topographical map of Africa—made almost completely from recycled materials—that would illustrate the continent's endangered habitats and species.

Friday was at Rachel's computer poking the keyboard and pointing to the letters as they appeared on the screen.

"Look at him type," Mickey said, impressed. "Maybe he should write our report."

"I don't think Mr. DeFina would appreciate 'XX BWETG GGOO' as enlightening for Earth Day." Rachel pointed to the garbled letters on the screen. "But he does love that keyboard. And yesterday, I swear, I saw the word 'banana' in there."

"Well, you know what they say: Give a hundred chimps a hundred typewriters and they'll produce a novel."

"I don't know about a novel, but it was kind of cool. I mean, of all the words he could have accidentally typed, it was 'banana.'"

Friday "hoo-hoo'd"; it came out like a bullfrog grunt.

Mickey moved closer to examine the glut of letters. "Hey. Look there. Near the bottom of the screen. 'Banana'!"

"If you don't count the other letters attached to it," Brianne said, being irritatingly sensible.

What was on the screen was this: BANANABBAAN-NAAANNNAAA

"The first six letters spell 'banana,'" Rachel said defensively.

Friday "hooted" and jumped up and down affirmatively.

"He does recognize that word," Mickey observed.

"He's a banana-holic. You want to see something?" She shouted, "Jared! Bring in your launcher. And have it loaded."

"Be right there!" he called from the hall.

She never had to ask her brother twice to show off any of his inventions. Requests for taking out the garbage, helping with the dishes, and feeding Wetspot were something else entirely—namely, lost causes.

Jared raced into the room (ordinarily off-limits when Mickey and Brianne were there) with a smile on his face and the long, banana-bearing cardboard tube in his hand.

Friday broke into an enthusiastic, anticipatory "uh-uh-uh" food bark.

"Ready. Aim"—Jared pushed the inner tube— "banana!" The fruit flew across the room straight into Friday's raised hand.

"Aw, right! He could be an outfielder for the Yankees," Mickey shouted as Friday peeled his catch.

"He could be a pitcher, too," Jared said. "Yesterday he was throwing a tennis ball across the living room for Wetspot."

"Not that Wetspot caught it," Rachel added, "but he did chase it."

"I hate to be the one to point this out," Brianne interrupted, not ever hating to be the one to point something out at all, "but the contest is next week. And we are NOT going to let Karla's mystery entry—whatever it is—win."

Rachel agreed. That's all they needed—to give Karla something else to feel superior to everyone about.

"Okay, okay. Jared, we have work to do." Rachel jerked her thumb toward the door. "And Friday, why don't you take a ride in the Upmobile." She handed him her Rubik's Cube to play with.

Friday scooted into the carton and hoisted himself up.

"All right, now let's—"

"Hey," Mickey said. "He . . . he, like, really understood you."

"I know," Rachel said, laughing, "and there wasn't even a banana involved."

"Can we just—"

"Relax, Brianne." Mickey held up his hand. "Rache, there's something really special about Friday. He's smart. I mean, he could be on TV."

"Why not his own series?" Brianne said, looking bored. When the spotlight wasn't on her, she let you know it.

My Chimp Friday 65

"We're supposed to keep him a secret, remember?"

"Well, he's not a secret. I know about him. Brianne knows. Mrs. Carey knows. The Animal Medical Center knows. And who knows who else knows?"

He was right, and Rachel knew it. Boy, he really irritated her when he brought up things she didn't want to think about—especially since she still didn't know *why* they had to keep Friday a secret in the first place.

"Well, he's staying a semisecret, then," she said stubbornly. "I mean, if people start asking questions about where we got him, they might take him back to that laboratory."

"I'm surprised your aunt Lisa hasn't already told the world." Mickey knew Aunt Lisa's reputation for spreading news faster than the Internet—particularly about things she wasn't supposed to.

"She doesn't know about Friday," Rachel explained. "It hasn't been easy keeping him under wraps, believe me. But it has been funny. I dress him in my Raggedy Ann doll clothes and wig, and she doesn't have a clue."

"I'd love to see that," Mickey said, laughing.

"Next time, Rachel will take a picture." Brianne was getting impatient. She disliked Karla more than Rachel did.

"Okay, let's get to work. Where are the little animals we're going to use?"

Brianne handed Rachel a box of tiny plastic animal figurines. There were leopards, tigers, elephants, ibex, gorillas, and three chimpanzees no larger than plums. Rachel had suggested Africa's animals, focusing on chimpanzees, as their project before Friday had entered her life, having read about their rapidly dwindling habitat in *Save the*

Planet. Now, holding a plum-sized chimpanzee in her palm, she felt a shiver at the back of her neck. Coincidences like this did that to her. But were they coincidences? Aside from being overly suspicious, she was also overly superstitious, a combination that worked for and against her, depending on the occasion.

She wasn't sure which way they were going quite yet.

The chimp in her palm looked a lot like Friday, with a tan face and a white fuzzy chin. It also looked very alone and out of place. Before she put it back in the box, Friday clambered down from the Upmobile and plucked it from her palm to examine it. He seemed bewildered.

"That's a chimpanzee . . . like you," Rachel said.

Friday pointed to himself questioningly. Rachel nodded. "Yes, you."

Friday looked at what he was holding. Then he studied the box for a long moment and carefully placed the figure back inside it.

They all leaned forward to see.

"Oh, man, this is too much," Mickey murmured.

Rachel felt another shiver at the back of her neck.

Friday had set the miniature chimp down—snugly and purposefully between the two other chimpanzees.

That night, Rachel had trouble falling asleep. She was worried about Friday's being lonely. Limiting a chimpanzee's extended family to Brianne and Mickey was, to say the least, limiting. She wished she knew how long they had to keep Friday a secret. Even more than that, she wished she knew why they had to keep him a secret in the first place. Finally, she wished she could just fall asleep. And she did.

10.

Plan B

Rachel suggested they bring their Honey, I Shrunk the Habitat exhibit to school the day before the contest in case it rained. Mickey and Brianne agreed. Mr. DeFina had said they could store it in the craft room but should cover it with something so it wouldn't be seen beforehand. He'd told them surprise was a powerful element and should never be underestimated. Rachel wasn't about to argue and brought a pink sheet from home.

Several sheet-covered exhibits were already in the room. Other students must have had rain on the brain, too. Tags with students' names and large DO NOT TOUCH signs on them were taped to the sheets. Some of the covered exhibits were oddly shaped. Karla Nesmith's was one of them.

"I'd love to take a peek at it," Brianne whispered.

"That's cheating," said Rachel, which was not to say she wouldn't have liked to peek, too, but she wasn't about to. You never felt as if you really won if you cheated. She'd learned that back in second grade when she was given first prize for a poem she hadn't written. It was a mistake she would never make again, and one that had taught her a life lesson she'd never forgotten. Whenever someone would mention that prize, she would feel sick to her stomach.

"I'm not a judge," Brianne protested. "Besides, I don't like surprises."

"That's not the point. You know the rules. No peeking at other students' projects."

"I'll bet if no one were around, Karla would peek at all of these."

"You'd probably win the bet, too," Mickey said, taping a DON'T EVEN THINK ABOUT IT! sign to Rachel's pink sheet.

As they were walking out, Rachel had that funny feeling at the back of her neck again. "Do you think it's safe to leave it here?"

"You are so suspicious," Mickey chided. "Relax. What's going to happen to it? Nobody's going to steal it."

"You're right. I just want Honey, I Shrunk the Habitat to win."

"We'll check on it before we go home today"—Mickey grinned—"worrywart."

"I am not a worrywart," snapped Rachel, grudgingly suspecting that she might be.

"Are, too."

"Am not!"

The bell rang, and they raced down the hall to homeroom.

When they opened the door to the craft room that afternoon, Rachel's jaw dropped, and she let out a scream more bloodcurdling than any she'd ever heard in a horror movie.

Their Honey, I Shrunk the Habitat project was indeed right where they had left it. But it was not *how* they had left it. The pink sheet was crushed, along with everything beneath it, under a heavy industrial pole lamp that lay across it like a fallen redwood.

Mrs. Holland, the school nurse, came running in. She was as white as her uniform. "What's happened?"

"There's been a terrible accident," Rachel said, dazed.

"Who's hurt? Where? Speak, child." Mrs. Holland looked as if she were going to swat Rachel to get her to talk.

Rachel pointed to the crumpled sheet pinned under the lamp. "That's our . . . that *was* our project."

"Your project? Your PROJECT! I thought someone was seriously hurt. You scared the daylights out of me with that scream, young lady. Don't you ever do that again. Do you hear me?"

Rachel nodded dumbly.

"A scream like that could give someone a heart attack." Mrs. Holland patted her chest with relief. "Remember that," she warned, walking stiffly back to her office.

"This is terrible," moaned Rachel.

"Worse."

"How could an accident like this happen?"

"It couldn't. There's no way this lamp *fell* down," Mickey said angrily, rolling the heavy metal base to the side. "Someone tried to make it look like an accident."

The three of them stared in disbelief at the remains of their project.

"It's ruined," Rachel said tonelessly. She bent over what was left of the green felt African veldt as if hypnotized, staring at the smashed pieces of corrugated cardboard, twigs and green plaster of paris that had been the Serengeti Plain. Every section of their topological green felt veldt had been destroyed. Tiny plastic animals lay scattered and broken. She picked up one of the plum-sized chimps. It was scratched, but still whole. She cradled it in her palm.

"Who do you think would do something like this?"

Brianne's eyes narrowed. "I don't have to think. I know."

"Karla?"

"Karla." Brianne snarled the name.

"What should we do?"

"We'll ruin hers." One thing about Brianne—she could make fast decisions. Maybe not smart ones, but she could make them fast.

"What's that going to get us?"

"Revenge."

"In trouble."

"Whoa!" Mickey said. "Just because Karla doesn't like us and we don't like her doesn't mean she would be this out-and-out destructive—does it?"

Rachel and Brianne nodded. "It does!"

"But we can't prove it."

"I know. So what do we do? Say a pole lamp accidentally destroyed our project? That's like saying 'the dog ate my homework.'"

"We still have our report and some pictures," Brianne offered.

"Oh, that's really terrific," Mickey snapped. "Entries are judged on originality and humor. So what do we do? Tell people to look at our pictures from the opposite end of a telescope to illustrate how habitats are shrinking?"

Rachel sat down beside the remains of the project, rolling the plum-sized chimp idly between her palms. The competition was less than twenty-four hours away, and their hopes of winning were . . . well, hopeless.

There had to be something they could do, but her brain seemed to have gone blank. Idly she tossed the tiny chimp figurine back and forth from one hand to the other.

"Too bad we don't have a Plan B," Mickey grumbled.

At which point a brilliant idea dropped into Rachel's lap. "I think I've got it!" she cried excitedly.

"Got what?"

"Plan B!"

Hester Mundis

11.

Exhibit Ape

The next morning, Jared shook his head as he watched Rachel stuff bananas and raisins into the zippered pockets of her backpack. "I don't think Dad's going to like this."

"That's why I didn't tell him, dummy. Would you hand me that Rubik's—hey, no, Friday." Rachel pushed his hand away and zipped the pockets closed. "Those are for later. And see"—she showed him the Rubik's Cube—"I'm bringing this for you to play with." Which was true, but she was also bringing it for luck. Something told her she was going to need a lot of it.

It was Jared.

"Lots of luck," he said when she explained her plan to sneak Friday into school to use as their exhibit for the contest.

"Friday likes riding in my backpack." She put it on and squatted down next to him. "Come on, get in."

Friday "hoo-hoo'd" noisily—sounding more like a cat with a hairball than an excited chimp—and climbed in.

Rachel stood and adjusted the straps as Friday bobbed up and down. "See? He likes it in there. He thinks it's a ride." She flipped the flap over his head.

"It looks as if your backpack has a motor in it. How are you going to explain a moving backpack?"

"I'll say it has a motor in it."

"And you think they'll believe that?"

"If I say there's a chimpanzee in there, do you think they'll believe that?"

Jared agreed she had a point. It wasn't easy to get him to agree when her reasoning was specious. S-p-e-c-i-o-u-s, she spelled automatically. She wished she could get that stupid word out of her head. It was really annoying. It was like a song that had gotten stuck in her brain.

Rachel looked at the clock. Mickey and Brianne were meeting her outside the school at eight. That would give her twenty minutes to get there.

She had Jared push a sweater and a small blanket on either side of Friday to keep him from bouncing around too much. It wasn't a seat belt, but it would have to do.

"I hope you know what you're doing," Jared said.

"Don't be a pessimist."

"What's a pessimist?"

"A wet blanket who sees failure instead of success at every turn. A doom and gloomer."

"I'm not a doom and gloomer."

He looked really miffed. "All I said was that I hope you know what you're doing."

"Well, I do," she assured him, feeling more confident by saying so. "We're going to show snooty Karla 'Rich Witch' that despite her lower-than-a-snake sneak attack, Honey, I Shrunk the Habitat is still in the running." Rachel decided they shouldn't change the name of their entry. Aside from having thought the name up herself, and quite proud of having done so, Mickey and Brianne agreed it was clever and likely to score points because of it. Besides, it still fit Plan B. After all, what more brilliant way to demonstrate the plight of animals whose natural environment was shrinking than to bring in a real, live endangered creature.

Marching toward the door with Friday bouncing in the pack on her back, Rachel shouted "good-bye" as if she were off to Kenya.

Friday, she was sure, was going to knock everyone for a loop.

She had no idea how right she was.

The Dahl Riverside School was seven long blocks from Rachel's apartment building. They seemed even longer with Friday jiggling on her back. Every time he tried to peep out, she had to reach around and flip the flap back over his head. "Just stay down. Okay? Is that so much to ask?"

She heard a muffled "hoo-hoo" from between her shoulder blades.

At the entrance to the school, a group of students crowded through the door. More stood around on the sidewalk. Mr. DeBelle, the security guard, watched from the steps. He was a funny-looking old man. His thin gray hair always looked to Rachel like strands of spaghetti combed over his head, and the fuzz that sprouted from his ears made him appear to have grown his own earmuffs. He stayed outside before classes to make sure no fights broke out and that none of the kids talked to strangers or started trouble. A lot of students called Mr. DeBelle "Mr. Dumb-bell," but it wasn't because he was stupid. It was just that the name always got a laugh.

Mickey and Brianne waved as Rachel approached.

"Plan B is in the bag," Rachel whispered, jerking her thumb toward the backpack.

"Can he breathe okay in there?" Brianne asked.

"Of course he can."

"Ouch!" Friday's hand had snaked out from under the flap and had a grip on Brianne's hair.

"Let go, Friday," Rachel hissed.

Mickey tucked Friday's arm back under the flap. "Do you think you'll be able to keep him hidden for another hour?"

The surprise factor would give them their best shot at scoring points, especially with Mr. DeFina. Their plan was to announce the exhibit. Brianne would read their report on shrinking habitats while Mickey held up photographs. Then, when it would appear as if Rachel was going to hand Mickey another photograph, she'd pull a real chimpanzee out of her pack.

"I'm going to try—uh-oh, here comes the pick of the litter herself."

"Litter box," Brianne muttered.

Karla Nesmith was walking in their direction, looking steadily ahead—no expression on her face at all. When she was about two feet from them, she tossed her head, flipping her long blond hair off her face. Karla always tossed her hair back like that. She did it a lot. She'd toss it whenever she stopped walking or talking or before doing either. And if someone else was talking, she'd do it more often. Her hair was always in motion. It was perfectly cut, long, silky, and blond. It was movie star hair, and Rachel hated her for it. It belonged on a head that deserved it.

"I heard what happened to your entry. So sorry."

Karla's lips barely moved when she spoke. Rachel wondered if it had something to do with having perpetual motion hair. "Accidents are always so"—she seemed to be searching for the perfect word—"so *unexpected.*"

"Duh," said Brianne under her breath.

"I wouldn't let it bother me if I were you. It's just a dumb school contest, anyway. If I didn't have to enter it, I wouldn't. Who cares about winning, anyway?" With that, she tossed her hair and went inside.

Mickey and Rachel looked at each other, the same thought occurring to both of them. Karla Nesmith was an out-and-out liar.

"How she could say that with a straight face?"

"Easy. She has two of them."

Rachel felt a commotion between her shoulder blades. "What's going on back there?"

Mickey laughed. "He's peeking out. Hi, guy."

Friday "hoo-hoo'd" softly. It was as if he knew he was supposed to be hidden. Just the top of his head and face were visible as he turned from side to side. His brown eyes widened as he looked around.

"I don't want him to get too excited." Rachel turned so that the back of the pack faced the wrought-iron fence protecting the small patches of grass and two trees that flanked the school's entrance. It seemed like the best way to keep Friday quiet.

She couldn't have been more wrong.

Friday's screech was so piercing and so unexpected that Rachel's startled scream was almost as loud. A large, gray squirrel had jumped from a tree to the top of the fence facing Friday and, never having seen a squirrel before, he freaked. Lips skinned back in a fearsome grimace, he unleashed an earsplitting crescendo of what had to be the most raucously strident of his thirty-two distinct sounds. The squirrel, now equally freaked and terrified, began squeaking nonstop, too.

"Hey! What's going on over there?" one of the students shouted.

"What's happening?" called another.

"Maybe it's a fight?"

A couple of students started toward them.

"EEEEEEKKKKKKKKK!" Brianne shrieked at the top of her lungs, momentarily drowning out Friday and the squirrel. "There's a rat in the gutter!" She pointed and shrieked again. "There! There!"

Rachel had to give it to Brianne: She really could make fast decisions. And sometimes they worked. This was one of those times.

The students ran toward the gutter.

"Where?"

"Is that it?"

"Wait. I think I see it."

Friday gave another loud screech. And so did Brianne. "There! Over there!" She pointed in the opposite direction.

The squirrel was gone, but now Brianne's screeching was freaking out Friday. He was chugging out a string of continuous "uh-uh-uhs." He sounded like The Little Engine That Couldn't.

"Shhhush," Rachel whispered. But there was no way to shush a chimp who didn't want to be shushed—and at the moment, Friday didn't want to be.

"I think we might have to rethink our plan B. At least the surprise part."

Hester Mundis

Just then Mr. DeBelle came storming down from the steps. "All right. That's enough of that noise. All of you. Right now. Inside—or I'm taking names!" He narrowed his eyes and pointed menacingly at them. The students grumbled as they turned and headed inside.

"Wow," murmured Rachel, "saved by DeBelle."

12.

Swinging into Action

Rachel's desk was across the aisle from Brianne's and in front of Mickey's. It was, she thought, a good setup for keeping her backpack—and its contents—out of view. She held it in her lap, covered with her sweater, and slipped Friday a banana.

"As I was saying," Mr. DeFina said, "this competition will be—"

The backpack gave a happy "uh-uh" food bark.

"Uh-oh," Mickey said.

Brianne launched into a coughing fit.

"Are you okay?" Mr DeFina looked concerned.

"Fine," Brianne said, holding her hand up. A good thing, too, Rachel thought. Mr. DeFina was kind of an overeager Heimlich maneuver giver. He'd already given it to two students who weren't actually choking. To be fair, though, he had saved the life of a man in McDonald's who was choking on a French fry. It made the papers because the man was the mayor's brother. Mr. DeFina's motto was, "Better *save* than sorry."

"Some of you have worked alone, others in teams. But

all of you—at least those of you who want a passing grade—have brought in something to increase awareness of how we can help protect our planet. We'll be going to the gym in a few minutes, and I want to remind you that there are to be no"—he paused in a way that signaled the approach of one of his enriching words—"derogatory comments made about any project."

D-e-r-o-g-a-t-o-r-y, Rachel spelled silently. A fancy word for "putdown."

The backpack was squirming in her lap and tickling her. She giggled.

"Inappropriate laughter will also be construed as"—that pause again—"a derogatory response."

Rachel held her breath and tried not to giggle, but she was just too ticklish. Muted giggles escaped like tiny burps, which sounded worse.

Mr. DeFina flashed her a stern look.

She nodded and covered her mouth.

Brianne took one look at Rachel, and she began to giggle. Sheila Edelstein, who sat in front of Brianne, and wasn't even looking at Rachel, heard Brianne, and she started to giggle. And then Julie Wheeler, who had the weirdest giggle in the world, giggled, and suddenly the whole class, even Karla, was swept into a serious case of The Giggles.

"All right. Get it out of your systems. Right now."

For the next five minutes the class was convulsed in giggles. They'd die down, but then someone would let one escape, and suddenly everyone was giggling again. And the more they tried to stop, the more they giggled.

"I think that's about enough."

Rachel didn't know why, but somehow this struck the

entire class—herself included—as hilarious, and they broke into uncontrollable laughter.

Mr. DeFina rapped on the desk with his fist, but the laughter continued. It was a good thing, too, because Friday was "hoo-hooing" lustily from Rachel's backpack.

The gym was decorated with Earth Day posters that students had made and were using as entries in the competition. Eddie Schecter—one of the boys Mr. DeFina had unnecessarily Heimlich maneuvered—had drawn a poster showing pesticide being sprayed on an apple (which, Rachel recalled, was what Mr. DeFina had thought Eddie had been choking on). It said: DON'T POLLUTE MY FRUIT!

The poster beside it was Shelly Talish's ABCS OF PCBS. It was a colorful alphabetical listing (with a pronunciation guide) of the chemicals that were contaminating rivers. It was, Rachel thought, beyond boring—but, then, so was Sheldon Talish.

Cole Mennell, a friend of Mickey's, had a huge display of products in the far corner of the gym—everything from sporting equipment and clothing to greeting cards and jewelry—all made from recycled materials. It made Rachel wonder if there were still things being made from scratch.

The refreshment table was next to it. Along with containers of juice and milk, there were platters of bagels, brownies, and bran muffins, with extra bags of each for refills. Almost all the students wanted brownies. The teachers—for some reason Rachel couldn't understand—seemed to favor bran muffins. Who'd choose a bran muffin over a brownie?

The first exhibit called was Burton Burdon's. B. B. was the smallest boy in Rachel's class, maybe even in the entire

Hester Mundis

school. Some kids said he was so small, his hair smelled like socks. But everyone liked him. He brought in a bicycle with a wagon full of cans, bottles, and tied-up newspapers attached to it.

"Bicycle to recycle," he said, clearing his throat and staring up at the four teachers sitting at the judging table with Mr. DeFina. "You don't pollute the atmosphere with a bike, and you don't pollute the environment if you recycle. Remember this on Earth Day and every day." He nodded his head in a kind of a bow.

"Thank you, Burton."

"No competition there," Mickey said under his breath.

Rachel, Brianne, and Mickey were standing in a far corner of the gym, near a pile of folded floor mats. What was salvageable of their Honey, I Shrunk the Habitat green felt veldt was on the floor. Next to it, Mickey had set up an easel, with the pictures they were going to show when Brianne read their report. Rachel was staying behind it to keep Friday concealed.

Friday was behaving himself. Plying him with bananas and raisins was working. So far.

The next three exhibits were about how to substitute natural products for pesticides. Susan Shay's was the most interesting. She and her friend Sheila had brought in a clear plastic box filled with ants.

"Many people think the only way to get rid of ants is to spray them with poisonous products like these." She swept her hand like a game-show hostess across a table filled with cans of bug killers. "But they can be dealt with in a much more planet healthy way by using common household vinegar." At this point she opened the bottle of vinegar and poured it over the ants, killing them.

The teachers were out of their chairs as if someone had hot-wired them. Miss Underwood, who taught social studies, looked as shocked as if someone really had. You would have thought Sheila was destroying baby seals or something.

"Let's all thank Susan and Sheila," Miss Underwood said quickly, standing in front of the box of dead ants.

"They're not all dead," someone yelled, pointing. "That one's still moving."

"Gross."

"Yuck."

"Where'd you get the ants, Susan? From your pants?"

"That'll be enough of that," Mr. DeFina said. "Next!"

Karla Nesmith stood and tossed her hair. Then she pushed her covered display, which was on a rolling typing table, to the center of the gym.

"I can't wait to see what she's done for Earth Day."

"Especially since she thinks she owns it."

After another hair toss, Karla unwound a long extension cord and plugged it into an outlet in the wall behind the teachers' table. Then she turned the gym lights off. It got a little darker, but not much. What it did do was get everyone's attention.

"For Earth Day, I want to remind everyone that we should, we must"—she paused to see that she had the students' attention—"save the whales!" With that, and a flourish of her arm, she dramatically unveiled her exhibit.

"Ooooos" and "ahhhs" riffled throughout the gym.

Illuminated in a large blue globe on the table was a holographic replica of a humpback whale. The three-dimensional effect was impressive. Rachel had to admit that the humpback whale looked very real—even if it was only the size of an Idaho potato.

"Big deal," Brianne muttered. "It's an expensive hologram. Her father probably bought it for her. What kind of project is that? Like Karla cares about whales."

Rachel shrugged. "Maybe she does."

"If you gave her a penny for her thoughts about whales, you'd get change back!"

Karla tossed her hair. "We should save the whales because . . . because whales were here first. Also, because they're big. And we don't need them for food because there are lots of other things to eat. Oh, and they sing. Male humpback whales spend half of every year doing hardly anything but singing. It's kind of like they're on tour. We should never eat animals that sing—or go on tour. So this Earth Day, we should think about saving the whales."

"Thank you, Karla," Miss Underwood said. "Can someone turn the lights back on?" Someone did. "Next!"

Mickey pushed the easel to the middle of the gym. Rachel walked behind it, holding her backpack and Friday close to her chest.

Brianne cleared her throat. "Our project, which was ruined yesterday, was called Honey, I Shrunk the Habitat. But"—she shot a really smug look at Karla—"we're still calling it that. Throughout Africa, animals are becoming endangered because people are taking over their feeding and breeding grounds. For example, look at that."

Mickey put up a picture of water buffaloes around a dried-up waterhole. Then another of a bulldozer tearing down trees in a forest.

"Bor-ING," someone shouted.

Undeterred, Brianne continued. "So we shouldn't buy

anything with ivory. We should let snakes and lizards keep their own skins. And only animals should wear real fur. Rachel?"

"That's right," Rachel said loudly from behind the easel. "And to send the message out this Earth Day, we've brought someone with us today who could do it best."

There was a groan from one of the students. "Not a speech."

"None of that, now"—Mr. DeFina wagged his finger—"or out you go."

As Mickey placed a large photograph of chimpanzees searching for food up on the easel, Rachel came out from behind it. "And here he is!" she shouted, holding Friday up in the air with both arms as if he were a trophy cup.

The gym exploded with shouts and whistles. Some students stood on the benches and stomped their feet.

"It's a real chimpanzee!"

"Bring him here!"

"Sit down, I can't see."

Mr. DeFina and Miss Underwood, taken off guard by Friday's appearance, shouted for the students to calm down.

Friday looked at the crowd of cheering, shouting students and joined in with a rousing grunt, scream, and howl selection from his top thirty-two repertoire. There hadn't been that much noise in the gym since The Dahl School had taken the basketball championship from Upton, and their coach had punched Coach Wagner right in the nose.

Once the gym quieted down, Rachel carried Friday to a stool in front of the easel. "Now, Friday, show us who needs our help."

Friday stood and ran his hand slowly over the large

Hester Mundis

color photo of the chimps. Then he scratched his head and reached down into Rachel's backpack and pulled out a banana.

There was a wave of quiet "ahs."

He peeled it slowly and extended his arm as if he were trying to feed the small hungry chimp in the photo. Then he "hoo-hoo'd" softly. Sadly.

Yes! Rachel gave herself an inner high five.

For one moment, Miss Underwood looked as if she was going to cry.

But that vanished the next moment when Friday leaned over and pressed his lips to the photo, causing the students to break into cheers and wild applause.

Startled and surprised (and full of himself, Rachel decided later), Friday did what came most naturally to him: He went ape!

Before she could grab him, he was off and running, with the fifth, sixth, and seventh grades of The Dahl School screaming encouragement.

Like he needs it, Rachel thought as she chased him. "Friday, you get back here this minute!"

But Friday was not listening. He was scaling the rope ladder and "hoo-hooing" all the way. Halfway up, he held on with one hand and waved. It was a crowd-pleaser, all right. The squeals of delight were deafening.

Whatever Mr. DeFina and Miss Underwood were shouting was drowned out by the noise.

Climbing higher, Friday launched into a hand-over-hand aerial act across the ceiling pipes to the opposite end of the gym.

Mickey ran over and waved a banana at him, trying to coax him down.

My Chimp Friday

"He's banana-d out," Rachel said, winded, now regretting having pushed all those bananas on him earlier.

"Look, he's over there."

Rachel turned just in time to see Friday swing down on the refreshment table, grab a bag full of bagels, and take off up the rope again. Halfway up, he began to hoot. The students hooted back.

"He's showing off, and they're encouraging him," Rachel wailed. "He's not paying any attention to me."

"HOO-HOO-HOO-HOO!" It sounded like a team cheer.

Friday took out a bagel, examined it, and then tossed it like a Frisbee toward the basketball backboard. It was a slam dunk! The bagel went right through the hoop.

There were wild screams of delight.

Another bagel hit the backboard and scored.

There was a roar from the students.

"Rachel!" Mr. DeFina shouted. His voice did not have the ring of an "A plus" to it.

"He's just a little . . . excited," Rachel explained. "I think it was all the sudden yelling."

"The sudden what? I can't hear anything with all this yelling suddenly going on."

"I—never mind."

"This is an Earth Day celebration. Not a circus."

Friday was obviously oblivious to this. As far as he was concerned, it was his moment to shine and he was making the most of it. His bagel basketball had the students cheering and shouting, *"SWOOSH!"* with every slam dunk.

"I'll get him down," Rachel promised.

"Do it quickly. We need some"—he paused in his here-comes-an-enriching-word way—"*decorum* around here.

And we need it right n—OW!" A bagel bonked him on the head. "Ra-CHELLLL," he growled.

Rachel swallowed hard. "I'll have him down in a jiff." She forced a smile, and headed for the ropes.

"Friday," she scolded, "you get down here right now or"—she held up the Rubik's Cube—"you'll never play with this again."

He stopped hooting.

"And you can forget about the *computer*, too."

That got his attention. He started his slide down the rope. Rachel folded her arms and studied the Cube as if she couldn't care less what he did.

When he reached the bottom, he held his arms out to her to be picked up.

She narrowed her eyes. "Oh, sure, now that you've had your fun and I'm in hot water over my head."

He "hoo-hoo'd," keeping his arms outstretched.

Rachel gave him a long, hard look. Then she picked him up and, even though she was really angry at him (well, maybe not *really* angry), she gave him a big kiss.

Everyone applauded as if it were the end of a play— Mickey and Brianne, too. They obviously weren't thinking about the A plus that her Plan B had deep-sixed.

"Uh-oh!" Mickey exclaimed. "Don't look now, but maybe you'd better. Over there."

Standing in the doorway was the feared and fearless Ms. Gargon, their school principal (better known as Gargoyle to anyone who was called before her). She ran The Dahl School with an iron ruler. She took teachers to task almost as often as students, and was equally strict with both. You never wanted to incur her wrath—or, for that matter, even cross her path—if you could help it. In a

My Chimp Friday

former life, you just knew her favorite phrase had been, "Off with their heads."

"Why, Ms. Gargon . . ." Mr DeFina stammered. "I—"

"Yes? You what?" Her eyes were the color of frozen ink. She spoke softly, but nobody missed a word. The gym had grown silent.

"I—I—"

Oy! Oy! thought Rachel. Here it comes.

"What I want to know is who is responsible for this." With that, she marched toward Rachel. For a long moment, she stared at Friday. Then she chucked him under the chin with her index finger and broke into the biggest grin Rachel had ever seen. No one had ever seen Ms. Gargon smile before. It was quite a sight. She had more teeth than a zipper.

It could have been a trick smile, but it was too late for Rachel to double think. "Well, um, we um . . . I um"—it sounded as if she were speaking some sort of *um* language—"he, um . . . I, um . . . we, um, brought him in for our Earth Day presentation. We thought he could get the message about endangered animals out in a way that would leave a . . . um . . . a—"

"Lasting impression?" Ms. Gargon offered, arching an eyebrow. It looked like a caterpillar stretching.

Rachel nodded.

"They never discussed it with me," Mr. DeFina said quickly.

"Or me," Miss Underwood added.

"So this was all done on their own initiative. Well, well, well."

Well what? Rachel wondered. Detention? Suspension?

Ms. Gargon extended her hand to Friday. To everyone's

amazement—including Rachel's—he took it, and she shook it.

"Congratulations," Ms. Gargon said. "A message well sent. I have never seen Dahl School students this interested in any Earth Day project."

"But—" Miss Underwood began.

"Butt out," Mr. DeFina wisely whispered.

Then Ms. Gargon did something really amazing. She leaned over and said to Rachel, "Nor have I ever seen an Earth Day project as cute as this." She tickled Friday under the chin again. "A winner," she said, then nodded to the students and left.

Brianne and Mickey thumped Rachel's back. She thought she was going to faint. She couldn't believe what had just happened. Five minutes before, she wouldn't have given them a whisker of a chance for even getting a passing grade, and now they'd been declared winners by no less than the Gargoyle herself. Rachel took the Rubik's Cube from Friday and kissed it. No one could tell her that this wasn't a lucky charm.

She was going to find that out all by herself.

13.

Earth Dazed

On the way home that afternoon, Rachel felt as if she were walking on waves of meringue. Everything around and inside her seemed splendidly, stupendously sweet. She would never forget this Earth Day as long as she lived! Friday's bagel basketball blowout had suddenly turned her into the most popular kid in school. (More popular even than Georgie Hass, whom everyone liked because he told the best jokes and always had free doughnuts from his father's bakery.) Zachary Wagner, who was a term ahead of Rachel—and the best-looking boy in seventh grade—took a picture of her holding Friday holding a bagel. She'd acted as if it was nothing, but inside she was screaming, ZACHARY WAGNER WANTS A PICTURE OF ME! even though she knew it was Friday whose picture he wanted.

She didn't like to gloat (another *enriching word* of Mr. DeFina's), but it was hard for Rachel not to feel more than a little satisfaction about seeing how angry and jealous Karla was. To say she was not a good loser would be an understatement. If looks could kill, Rachel had no doubt she would be dead right now.

"I'll tell you something, Friday," she said, not caring who on the street saw her talking over her shoulder to her backpack, "having you is better than having long, silky, perfect movie star hair."

Friday poked his head out. A man passing by did a double take. Rachel laughed, juggling her Rubik's Cube from hand to hand. She couldn't wait to tell Jared and her father about how well everything had gone.

Turning the corner on Eighty-seventh Street, she saw that Pickle Nose was back again. He was sitting on the steps of a brownstone across the street, reading the newspaper. He should meet Aunt Lisa's friend, Wendy Mills, Rachel thought. They're both around here often enough. They could keep each other company.

Instead of going in the front entrance of the building, Rachel headed down the alley to the basement. It was a shortcut that she and Jared took when they were in a hurry, because the service elevator was just to the left at the foot of the steps.

Whistling, she rubbed her Rubik's Cube. This was the luckiest day of her life. She wished she could come up with an idea that would enable her to take Friday to school more often.

Just as she wished this, a lightbulb went on in her head. But before she could even think about her idea, there were footsteps behind her. Someone grabbed her shoulder. The next thing she knew, her backpack was wrenched from her, and she was falling down the stairs.

Distantly she heard Friday screaming and a dog barking, both rapidly getting fainter. She wondered what that idea was that she'd had.

And then everything went black.

My Chimp Friday

When she opened her eyes, her head was in the crook of Mr. Aplox's arm, and something was licking her face. It was Attila, Mr. Aplox's rottweiler. She closed her eyes. Attila the Killer licking her face? She had to be dreaming.

Mr. Aplox gave her a little shake. "Are you okay? Who were those men?"

Rachel reopened her eyes. The pain on the side of her head was no dream. She touched the spot. It was warm and sticky with blood. Attila tried to lick it again, but Mr. Aplox pushed him away and dabbed at her head with a cloth.

"What men?" Rachel looked around. Her backpack was lying beside her. It was empty. She screamed. "FRI-DAY!"

"Thursday," Mr. Aplox corrected. "Take it easy."

"Where's Friday? FRIDAY!"

Mr. Aplox looked confused. "Tomorrow is Friday."

"No, Friday is a chimpanzee. He was in my backpack, and now he's . . . he's been chimp-napped!"

"A chimpanzee in your backpack?"

"It was Earth Day. He was our Plan B. He—oh, never mind." It hurt to try to explain. "I don't even know what happened."

"Well, after you fell—"

"You mean, after I was pushed."

"I guess. I didn't see that. I heard it, though. Two men came running through the basement and Attila lunged for them. It was dark, but it did look as if one was holding a monkey and—"

"He's an ape."

Hester Mundis

"Well, whatever it was, Attila must have suspected monkey business, because he lunged and the guy tripped, and the . . . whatever he was carrying got away."

"Away? Away where?" Rachel was on her feet. "Friday! Fri-DAY!"

"Most likely he's frightened and hiding."

"We have to find him!"

"First I think we ought to take care of that cut on your forehead."

"It's nothing," Rachel said. She said it because that's what she thought she ought to say; that's what people in the movies always said when things like this happened. They said it was nothing even if it was a bullet wound. She would never call a bullet wound "nothing." She hoped she'd never have to.

The basement of the building was dimly lit, especially the storage bay area, which had only a few bare bulbs in wire cages for illumination.

"He could be anywhere," Mr. Aplox pointed out. "There are a lot of nooks and crannies down here."

For a moment, Rachel wondered what a "cranny" really was and if it could exist without a "nook." She'd never heard of anyone looking in "every cranny." There was always a "nook" involved. But whatever a cranny was, she knew it was small—small enough for a chimpanzee to hide and get hurt in.

"Oh, Mr. Aplox," Rachel wailed. "We have to find him."

Attila sat down. The canine terror of Eighty-seventh Street looked bored.

"Say, I have an idea. Attila might be able to help us. Do you have anything that has the chimp's smell on it?"

My Chimp Friday 95

"He doesn't smell," Rachel said defensively. Why did people always think that about apes?

"I mean his scent. Dogs have a sense of smell that is a million times more powerful than humans'. Attila can always find his toys no matter where I hide them."

Rachel was more amazed that a dog like Attila played with toys than the fact that he could find them. She handed Mr. Aplox the blanket and sweater that had bolstered Friday in the backpack.

"Here, Attila." Mr. Aplox held the blanket under the dog's nose. Attila sniffed. Then he sniffed the sweater. "See, he's getting the scent."

Attila went back and forth between the sweater and the blanket. Then he went to the backpack and sniffed.

"What's he doing now?"

The massive rottweiler had put his head all the way into the backpack.

"He's getting the full whiff," Mr. Aplox said, at which point Attila emerged with half a bagel and promptly ate it.

Mr. Aplox coughed. "Come on, boy." He put the blanket under the dog's nose. "Find him! Find that little monkey!"

"Ape," corrected Rachel.

Attila raised his head. He scrunched his muzzle as he sniffed.

"Ready, boy?" Mr. Aplox unhooked Attila's leash and pointed to the morass of nooks and crannies that lay beyond the storage bays. "Find him!"

The huge black-and-tan dog took off with his nose in gear. He was sniffing everywhere. He ran from the bicycle rack to the storage bays and back again. Then he headed toward the far side of the basement and was lost from sight.

 Hester Mundis

"Friday! FRIDAY!" Rachel called.

"WOOF, WOOF, WOOF!" Attila's barks were coming from behind the boiler in the darkest part of the basement.

Mr. Aplox grabbed a flashlight. "Come on."

The dog was sitting below a narrow, porthole-sized air shaft on the other side of a fence-high partition that separated the storage bays. Mr. Aplox shined the flashlight at it, but there was nothing there. "False alarm." They started back.

Attila barked again. Then there was another bark—from the air shaft! It sounded like a seal with a fish stuck in its throat—one of Friday's top ten of his thirty-two. Rachel would recognize it anywhere.

"Friday! It's okay, you're safe!" Rachel screamed. "It's me. Come out!"

Friday's fur-bristled head peeked out tentatively, moving cautiously to the left and then to the right. Then he looked down and saw Attila. He made a noise that sounded like a cross between a bark and a burp.

Attila looked up, looked interested. Friday gave another bark-burp, then slowly stretched his hand down toward the dog.

Rachel opened her mouth to cry out a warning "don't!" But then the most extraordinary thing happened. Attila began licking Friday's hand—just licking it—and not as if it were an appetizer. He was just giving Friday's palm an old-fashioned, friendly dog licking.

"Looks like Attila's found a friend," Mr. Aplox said, chuckling, "and you've found your chimp."

Friday scampered to the floor and climbed onto the partition. He waved to Attila and then jumped into Rachel's arms, hooting.

My Chimp Friday

Attila followed, leaping over the partition and wagging his entire body. "Good work, boy." Mr. Aplox rubbed the dog's head vigorously.

"Thank you, Attila," Rachel said, never meaning a thank-you more. She hugged Friday so tightly that he squealed. Neither of them cared.

As Mr. Aplox helped her gather the contents of her damaged backpack, Rachel saw him pick up her Rubik's Cube. Some lucky charm, she thought.

"You're one lucky girl," he said, handing it to her.

"Lucky?"

He pointed to where the Cube had been. "Very lucky." There, right where her head had landed when she'd fallen, was an iron spike sticking out of the concrete. "All that came between you and the big dirt nap was that Cube."

The big dirt nap! Mr. Aplox didn't mince words. Rachel gazed at the Cube. All the colors were lined up perfectly. Maybe her stupid superstitions and suspicions weren't so stupid after all. That funny prickly feeling was creeping up the back of her neck again.

"Those guys were after the chimp. Probably figured they could sell him for a lot. Your father should probably report it to the police. They could be a—"

Mr. Aplox was cut off by the sound of high heels running down the steps. The woman wearing the high heels stopped short when she saw them, as if they weren't the people she expected to see. "Oh," she said.

Uh-oh, thought Rachel.

It was Aunt Lisa's friend, Wendy Mills, "the catch" stalker.

Attila growled. Wendy Mills backed toward the brick wall and stiffened.

"*Aus!*" Mr. Aplox shouted. It was a German word meaning "out," which he had once explained to Rachel, was like a big "NO!" Mr. Aplox also used German words to tell Attila to "sit" (*sitz*) and "stay" (*bleib*), which made no sense to Rachel since neither Mr. Aplox or Attila were German. It made even less sense, since Attila generally did what he wanted to do, anyway.

"I was passing by and I thought I heard . . . a commotion," Wendy Mills said. "My goodness . . . what is that you're holding?" Her eyes widened as she looked at Friday. "Is that a chim-pan-zee?" She pronounced it as if it were some sort of Chinese food, like moo-shu-pork.

"Yes. But please don't tell my aunt about him. It'll just make her crazy and she'll drive us crazy."

"Your aunt?" The woman batted her eyelashes innocently.

"You don't have to pretend. I know that you're my aunt Lisa's friend Wendy Mills. And I know why you've been hanging around here, too."

"Oh, really?"

"To check out my father."

"Your father?

"Yes, my father," Rachel said in an exasperated way, "'the catch.'"

"Ah, 'the catch.'" Wendy nodded. "I didn't know I was so . . . transparent."

"I figured out who you were a week ago. I'm overly suspicious," Rachel confessed, "so I noticed you right away. And then when Aunt Lisa told me about what she'd told you to do, I put one and one together and . . . well, there you were. Or here you are."

"My, my. I guess there's no fooling you, Miss Nancy Drew."

"It's Rachel," she said, embarrassed.

"Well, I'm pleased to meet you, Rachel." The bracelet on Wendy's wrist jingled as she extended her hand.

Rachel shook it and saw that the jingle came from two swinging gold initials, a **W** and an **M,** dangling from the bracelet. It wasn't difficult to be Nancy Drew with clues like that.

Friday's arm brushed her forehead, and Rachel winced.

"You'd best go upstairs and take care of that cut. And tell your father about what's happened," Mr. Aplox advised.

"What did happen?" Wendy Mills looked concerned.

"Two men tried to chimp-nap my chimp."

"Why, that's terrible." She put her arm around Rachel.

"It would have been if they'd gotten him." Rachel felt her voice catch, as if she was going to cry.

"Maybe Ms. Mills can go upstairs with you, Rachel." He turned to Wendy. "She's kinda shook up."

"I can see that." Wendy Mills gave Rachel's shoulder a gentle squeeze. "I'll go with you."

"Thank you," said Rachel. "But I'd really rather that you didn't."

"Are you sure?"

Rachel nodded.

"Well, then, I guess I'll be going." Wendy turned to leave, then hesitated before starting up the stairs. "Really, you're sure now that you don't want me to come with you?"

Rachel assured her that she really didn't.

Really! Rachel had enough explaining to do to her

Hester Mundis

father about sneaking Friday out of the house in the first place without having to explain bringing home a friend of Aunt Lisa's who'd been secretly stalking him. If there was one thing she'd learned about her father's "saintly patience" it was that as "saintly" as it was, it only went so far. And she wasn't about to go there.

14.

Shopping Maul

WHAT?" Her father boomed. His face was dark and his lips tight. Rachel had never heard him boom before.

"We needed a Plan B, Dad. Friday was our only chance." She slid her foot back and forth on the carpet, not meeting his eyes.

"That's not the point. You should have asked me before you did something like that."

"Would you have let me take him to school?"

"Of course I would have. That's what's upsetting me. I wouldn't have thought of your being in any danger taking him to school."

"It happened on her way home," Jared pointed out.

"And in broad daylight."

"Maybe I was wrong. Maybe Bucky wasn't being 'overly dramatic,'" her father said, stroking his chin. "Maybe there is some reason we have to keep Friday a secret."

"What do you think it is?"

"Do you think it's top secret?" Jared asked eagerly.

"It's top secret to me." Ben Stelson shrugged. "I just

don't know. Then again, what happened this afternoon could be just a coincidence, a fluke. Those guys may have seen you as an easy target and Friday as something they could turn over for quick cash."

"They might break into our apartment to try to steal him," Jared said.

"They don't know what apartment we live in."

"Maybe they followed you."

"Nobody followed me," Rachel said. Boy, and she thought she was suspicious.

"I'm not taking any chances. I'm building a booby trap."

Rachel rolled her eyes. "Not another one!" The last time Jared built a booby trap was after the Wallersteins' apartment had been robbed. It was a device that, if triggered, would spill flour on the thieves, causing them to leave a trail that police would be able to follow. Unfortunately, Aunt Lisa had triggered it by mistake. She had gotten a flour shower that made her look like the ghost of Christmas past, and Jared and Rachel had been grounded for a week.

"This is going to be a root beer booby trap. Sixty-four fluid ounces of prevention."

"Just make sure not one of those ounces come in contact with Aunt Lisa, or this time we could be grounded for life."

The attempted chimp-napping didn't cause any lessening of Friday's natural exuberance. If anything, he seemed to be more outgoing, more curious, and more intelligent than before. Over the next few days, Rachel searched the Internet for more information about chimpanzees. There was quite a lot of speculation about what they were and weren't capable of doing. But what she found out beyond a shadow of a doubt was that Friday was definitely smarter than your average ape.

Almost unbelievably smarter.

He could now play solitaire on the computer, right through to the aces, and win. After two afternoons of showing him flash cards with the alphabet on them, he could pick out the letters on the computer keyboard. He could even make a phone call if Rachel wrote the number down. Mickey was knocked out when he answered the phone and heard Friday's "hoo-hoo" hello.

"And he pushed the buttons himself," Rachel exclaimed proudly.

"Chimp-tastic."

"You'd better believe it. He solves that Rubik's Cube every time. And he's interested in everything."

Friday and Jared were sprawled on the floor across from each other, a chessboard between them. Friday was sucking on one of the pieces.

"Friday, take that pawn out of your mouth!" Rachel yelled. "Sorry. Jared is teaching him to play chess."

"Next you're going to tell me that he can play the piano."

"No," Rachel drawled, "but he can change a lightbulb. Didn't even need a ladder to do it."

"Are you sure he's a chimpanzee?" Mickey laughed.

"I'm sure. And that's sort of why I'm calling. I've noticed that he's spending a lot of time in front of the computer looking at pictures of chimpanzees. It's just kind of—oh, I don't know—like he's . . . well, he runs his fingers

Hester Mundis

over the pictures and sometimes leans forward to kiss the screen. I think he needs some company. He may be lonely surrounded by all us hairless humans."

"Wetspot's not hairless, and he's not human," Jared pointed out.

Rachel shushed him.

"Wait a minute," Mickey said. "You're not suggesting getting another chimp to keep him company?"

"Nope. The next best thing."

"What's the next best thing?"

"One of those realistic Steiff chimp dolls. They look as if they can really eat bananas. Come with me to FAO Schwarz this afternoon and I'll show you. I think Friday would love it."

"You want Friday to come with us?"

"Sure. Why not?" she said, knowing very well.

"After what happened—"

"There'll be two of us. Besides, things like what happened happen every day in this city. I'm not going to become paranoid. I don't want to suspect there are people out there who are *after* Friday." Unfortunately, she did suspect it. But she didn't want to.

She also didn't want to keep Friday grounded and confined to the apartment because she was paranoid. Which she now suspected that she was.

And so did Mickey Phelps.

"If you're not paranoid, then why do we have to disguise him?" Mickey asked as he helped Rachel put the Raggedy Ann dress and red wig on Friday before they left that afternoon. Friday thought it was a hoot and kept running to the mirror to look at himself, making guttural

My Chimp Friday

clicking noises that sounded like stifled giggles or something caught in his throat.

"We don't have to advertise him, either. Girl carrying backpack with Raggedy Ann doll doesn't attract attention. Girl carrying chimp is another story." She put the pack on, and Mickey put Friday in.

The ride in the bus across town was uneventful, with a minor exception—a two-year-old boy. As they were getting off, Friday stuck his head out of the backpack and smiled at a toddler, unaware that his friendly flash of teeth could be misinterpreted. A scream of such terror broke from the little boy that the bus driver stopped and stood up to see what was happening. Everyone glared at the child's mother, who looked very confused—and then also burst into tears.

FAO Schwarz, which is New York City's most impressive toy store and a major tourist attraction, was crowded with shoppers when Mickey and Rachel got there.

"I don't think anyone's going to notice us," Rachel whispered. "The kids are all looking at toys, and the parents are all looking at prices."

They quickly headed for the store's huge jungle display of lifelike stuffed animals. It was huge and impressive. There were chimps hanging from trees; chimps eating bananas; chimps rolling around and riding on one another's backs. It reminded Rachel of last-year's Dahl School picnic at Bear Mountain State Park.

"I want Friday to pick the doll," Rachel said. "So let's give him a choice. Hold one up and let him see it. Make sure no one sees him. Then hold up another. He'll let you know which one he wants."

"How will he do that?" Mickey asked.

"Just watch."

Mickey shrugged and lifted a chimp doll to the backpack so Friday could see it. "This one?"

Friday cocked his red-wigged head to one side.

Mickey pushed Friday back down and picked up another doll. "Or this one?"

Friday had no problem with decisions. Before you could say, "hoo-hoo," or "how," he'd grabbed the doll and pulled it into the backpack.

"Well, that was easy," Mickey said.

"Don't be so sure. Now you have to take it from him so we can pay for it."

"Yo, Friday," Mickey whispered to the backpack. "We have to pay for your little pal." He reached in and pulled out the doll.

Friday reached out and pulled it back in.

"He doesn't want to give it back," Mickey said.

"Friday, they'll think we're shoplifting. Now give it to Mickey."

Mickey tried again to retrieve it, and again Friday pulled it back.

"Just take it from him," Rachel said, exasperated.

"He's not going to like it."

"He'll like it less if we get arrested and he's hauled off to a zoo."

"Okay. Here goes nothing." Mickey reached in and snatched the doll before Friday could reach out. "Got it."

Looking like a discarded Halloween toy in his Raggedy Ann wig, Friday sprang up in the backpack, let loose an angry round of "hoo-hoos," and grabbed another doll from the display.

"That's enough," Rachel scolded. She reached around and grabbed the doll from him. As she was putting it back, there was a screech from between her shoulder blades. "What the—" She felt a blow to her back and tumbled forward into the display.

Mickey crashed down beside her.

Another chimp-napping! Rachel scrambled to her feet in time to see Friday leap from beneath the leather jacket of the man who had grabbed him.

"He's getting away!"

Friday had pulled off his dress and wig and was heading back toward Rachel. The man in the leather jacket, red-faced and angry, was chasing him. Rachel knew she had to do something fast but she didn't know what, so she did what came naturally: She screamed at the top of her lungs. Then she hurled a chimp doll full force at the red-faced man headed toward her. Mickey hurled another.

"Two hits, no errors," Rachel shouted. "Keep 'em coming."

Shoppers turned to gape. Kids started to laugh.

"Hey, what's going on over there?" Two security guards ran toward the display area.

Friday dove headlong into the center of the pile of stuffed dolls. The man in the leather jacket pushed people aside and ran down the escalator. "Stop that man," Rachel shouted. "He's a . . . a chimp-napper."

The two security guards reversed direction and headed for the escalator.

Rachel's eyes widened. Standing off to the side was none other than that guy with the pickle nose—and once again he was wiping it on his jacket! Who was that creep? And what was he doing in FAO Schwarz?

"Mickey," Rachel whispered, "that weird guy who's been hanging around my apartment building is here."

"Where?"

"Right over"—she turned to point—"there . . ." Her voice trailed off. He was gone. "I'm sure it was him."

"You were *sure* it was going to be okay to take Friday, too."

"Okay, but"—she blinked suddenly—"wait a minute." There was a dark-haired woman in a blue pants suit heading toward the elevator. It was Aunt Lisa's friend Wendy. She was sure of it.

Or was she?

Suddenly Rachel wasn't sure what she was sure of anymore. But she sure wasn't going to let Mickey know it.

"Come on. We'd better get Friday and—"

A security guard's hand clasped Mickey's shoulder. "Okay, now what's this all about?"

"A man pushed us!"

"And he tried to steal our chimp"—Rachel hesitated, looking at the crowd that had gathered—"*doll*." She quickly picked one up and began petting it.

The guard shook his head. "A loony tune, probably. Sorry about that." He brushed his hands toward the crowd of gawking shoppers. "Everything's under control. Let's not block the aisle." Turning back to Rachel, he added, "You can pay for your animal at the cashier."

When the guard had gone, Rachel put the doll down on top of the others and looked around. "Where is Friday?" she whispered.

"He was in this pile a minute ago."

"I want THAT one! The one in the MIDDLE!" A little boy in a blue blazer was stomping his feet and pointing up

My Chimp Friday

at three chimps sitting on a branch in the fake tree at the center of the jungle display. Their arms were positioned so that they looked like "hear-no-evil, see-no-evil, speak-no-evil": The one on the left was covering his ears, the one on the right covering his eyes, and the one in the center, covering his mouth.

"They're all the same," his mother said, annoyed. "Let's go."

"I want THAT one. He moves."

Rachel and Mickey looked up. Speak-no-evil winked at them.

"None of them move," the boy's mother snapped. "Now take this doll, or—"

"I WANT THAAAAT ONE!"

"You'll take this one and like it!" And with that, she dragged the boy and a doll toward the cashier.

Friday dropped quietly from the tree onto the soft plush of chimp dolls. Rachel picked him up and hugged him. "Quickly," she said to Mickey, "put him in my backpack and give him a banana. Forget about the doll. And, Friday, you stay down in there. Okay?"

There was an affirmative "hoo-hoo." Friday took the banana—and a big bite out of it—before ducking beneath the flap.

An elderly woman had stopped in front of the display and was squinting as if to make sure she'd just seen what she had just seen. Then she shook her head, as if clearing it of such a ridiculous notion, and walked away.

As they were leaving, the security guard that had been upstairs was standing at the door. "Well," he said, glancing at her backpack, "I'm glad to see you got the doll that you wanted."

Hester Mundis

"Thank you," said Rachel, hurrying past him.

"You know, you could swear that thing is really eating a banana."

Rachel smiled. "I'm sure that I could."

15.

Package from a Dead Man

The following day a large, battered package arrived from Africa. B. GREENE was written in yellow Magic Marker in the upper left-hand corner, barely legible above an indecipherable address. The package looked as if it had gone through a giant omnivore's digestive system. As it turned out, it had gone through the U.S. Postal Service equivalent—an incorrect zip code.

"It's weird getting a package from a dead man." Rachel peered over her father's shoulder as he pulled the layers of tape off the box.

"He wasn't dead when he sent it," said Jared.

"Thanks, genius."

"Friday wants to see, too."

"I see that." Friday hung by one hand from the pole lamp beside their father's desk, craning his neck. He looked like a conductor hanging off the side of a San Francisco cable car.

"I can't imagine what Bucky would be sending us," Ben Stelson said as he opened the box.

"Neither can I," said Rachel. And even if she could, she

never would have imagined what was actually there. "Ohmygod." She groaned. "It's that big, ugly coat of his." Hadn't he ever heard of Goodwill?

Her father scratched his head. "Why on earth would he send us his coat? Wait a minute. There's a letter here."

"What does it say?"

"Read it."

"I will. I will. Take it easy. Where are my glasses?"

Rachel's father often asked that question, and the answer was almost as often the same: "They're on your head."

"Right." He cleared his throat. Rachel, Jared, and Friday leaned forward. "Here it goes: 'Dear friends, I'm sending you my coat for safekeeping. I can't explain why now, but you must keep it well hidden.'"

"No kidding," Rachel said. "Like we'd want to show it off."

"'And you must also continue to keep Mergatroid's whereabouts a secret.'"

Mergatroid. That stupid name again.

"'Because it may be a matter of'—" He stopped. His face had kind of a sickly look. The last time Rachel remembered seeing that look on her father's face was when he'd accidentally eaten one of Wetspot's dog treats.

"A matter of what?" she asked.

"'A matter,'" he said slowly, "'a matter of life and death.'"

"Now he tells us!"

Rachel hadn't said anything to her father about the second chimp-napping attempt at the department store the day before because she knew he would be upset and think that Friday was putting them in danger. Now he'd be sure of it. But there was no point in worrying him about some-thing that had already happened, was there? She'd just keep quiet and keep Friday off the street until the life-and-death matter didn't matter anymore. It would be okay. Friday would be fine. People had indoor cats, didn't they?

"Look!" Jared pointed. Friday had crawled into the box and was pulling the coat around him.

"It must remind him of Bucky. If it makes him happy, I guess I can keep the *thing* in my room—for a while." There was no way she was going to let a coat that ugly stay in her room on a permanent basis.

Friday rode on the coat as she and Jared dragged it to her room.

"This coat is REALLY heavy. I wonder how that little man could walk in it?" Rachel spread it out on the floor. "Look at the lining. It's as thick as a mattress."

Friday sniffed it, tasted it, then suddenly began tug-ging at it from under the inside of the sleeve.

"Hey. We're supposed to hide the coat, not shred it. What are you doing?"

Friday "hoo-hoo'd" excitedly, pointing to what looked like snaps in the fabric.

"He's trying to show us something. Those snaps."

Jared bent down for a closer look. "Whoa. Those aren't snaps."

"What are they?"

"They look like . . . connectors for something."

"In a coat?"

"I think this is more than a coat," Jared said, suddenly sounding very adult.

"Like, what more? What more can a coat be than a coat?" Especially one as ugly as Bucky Greene's.

"A computer," Jared said.

"Ah, 'Q,' you have such great ideas for James Bond."

"I'm not kidding, Rachel. I think there's a computer here somewhere."

"I wouldn't be surprised if there was a Volkswagen in there—Friday, stop that."

Friday tugged at the lining again, and there was the ripping sound of Velcro unattaching itself.

Jared and Rachel gaped. Their eyes were wide with disbelief, but there was no doubt about what they were looking at. Built into the coat was a computer almost as thin as a lasagna noodle.

"I see it but I don't believe it," said Rachel.

"Believe it." Jared put his hand in the sleeve and withdrew two slim wires. "Somehow his coat is hot-wired to his computer. There must be a silicon chip transponder in the coat."

"What does that mean?" Rachel asked. Jared was way ahead of her when it came to computers. An enriching Mr. DeFina word, "precocious," came to mind. (P-r-e-c-o-c-i-o-u-s.)

"It means that this is"—he plugged the wires into the connectors and a color LCD screen lit up above the inside pocket—"a working computer."

The screen was a pale blue. In the center was a box that said "Enter User Name and Password." The user name was already there in all capital letters. "BUCKY."

The cursor pulsed by the space for the password.

"Wow," Rachel said, "let's try GREENE." Friday watched as she typed.

An error message appeared. "PASSWORD INCORRECT."

"How about 'Mergatroid'?"

"Worth a try," said Rachel. But again the error message appeared.

For the next five minutes they tried password after password—from ape and chimpanzee to xylem (which Rachel remembered from a spelling bee) and Zaire (a country in Africa)—but none of them worked.

Rachel stood up, annoyed. "I never liked that coat."

Friday "hoo-hoo'd" like an owl with an idea and hunched over the keyboard.

"Hey!" Jared said, holding his hand back. "Be careful."

"Wait a minute. Wait a minute. Let him." Rachel said, struck by the way Friday was studying the keyboard; his index finger moving from left to right over the keys, without pressing them, as if it were a Ouija board.

Rachel had once used Brianne's Ouija board to see if she could contact her mother. The message that she thought it spelled made no sense. It was, "Hold tight with open arms." But she never forgot it.

"Look!"

As the two of them stared, Friday typed a **B**, then an **A**, then an **N**, than another **A**, then another **N**, and another **A**.

"Banana!" they breathed in unison.

Friday hooted proudly, his shoulders rolling up and down.

A list of files appeared on the screen. One of them was highlighted in yellow.

"'The Nana Banana Chronicles.' I wonder what that could be? I'm going to open it."

"Do you think we should?"

"I don't know, but I'm going to." And with that, Rachel did.

"Wow. Look at this. Look at this. It's all about his experiments. It's about bananas and Mergatroid"—she really hated that name—"and a 'nana banana' and DNA."

"What does it all mean?"

"How am I supposed to know," she said defensively.

"I'll get Dad."

Ben Stelson let out expressive "whews" after every few sentences he read.

"What?" Rachel asked. "What is it?"

"It's something very, very amazing," he said, with such seriousness that it sounded scary. "Remember I told you that Bucky was working on genetically engineered bananas?"

"Uh-huh. No-skid peels."

"He had also been working for quite a while on one that would stay ripe for a long time before turning brown. The 'nana banana' was the grandmother of these bananas. He discovered, after feeding it to a lab chimp, that it had the amazing side effect of increasing intelligence. Somehow—and I'm not quite sure how myself—the plant's genetically modified DNA mixed with the chimp's DNA, and the result was the production of a unique brain chemical that revved up the animal's IQ tremendously. He was quite sure it would work in humans, too."

"You mean anyone could eat these bananas and become a genius?"

"Theoretically, yes."

"Boy, anyone who didn't like bananas would be an idiot. In more ways than one."

"But he says when he found out that the owners of Bioallmeans, Mimi and Gary Wykaire, wanted this formula to

My Chimp Friday

sell to select groups in search of power, he destroyed it. His reasoning was—let's see, he says it here—ah, yes, 'Intelligence without wisdom can be extremely dangerous—especially in the wrong hands. And at Bio-allmeans there are some *very* wrong hands. The only evidence of my formula's existence now is in Mergatroid's DNA—and I have no doubt that people would tear this chimp apart to find how to replicate it. He must be guarded well.'"

"That explains why he wanted us to keep Merga"—Rachel caught herself—"Friday a secret."

Her father's brow furrowed, and the teepee-like lines above his nose deepened. "The last entry is dated the night that he came here. It says, 'Gary and Mimi Wykaire have no scruples. In fact, I fear Gary and Mimi Wykaire have ways of getting away with'—" He stopped and looked at Rachel with deep concern.

"Getting away with *what?*" she whined impatiently.

"Murder," he said.

Hester Mundis

16.

A Relative Unknown

As startling as the discovery of Bucky's computer in a coat was, it was just the tip of the banana, so to speak, where the huge garment was concerned. Further rummaging on Friday's part brought forth a file cabinet's worth of stuff.

"I can't believe all this could have been in there," Rachel said to Jared as Friday continued to pull papers, clippings, instruction booklets, receipts, and letters from the dozen pockets inside the coat like candy from a piñata.

"And I thought you carried a lot in your backpack."

"Look at this. It's a warranty for an electric can opener."

"You think that's in the coat, too?"

"I wouldn't be surprised."

Wetspot, totally unconcerned, lay in the doorway lazily cleaning his undercarriage.

The floor of Rachel's bedroom looked like they had just celebrated New Year's Eve. Her father had a small pile of letters beside him and was reading quietly. Too quietly, Rachel thought. "What are those?"

"Letters," he said, in a way that told Rachel he was thinking about how to say what he was about to say.

"Letters? From whom?"

"They're from a woman named Dee Dee VanAusdale, who is in charge of a wild chimp preserve in Kenya, where they're trying to reestablish the population."

"Kenya? Isn't that where Bucky went on his top secret mission—before his *accident?*"

"Yes, it was." He handed her the letters. "It seems that Mergatroi—er, Friday—and his sister were born in Africa and—"

"Friday has a sister?"

Her father nodded. "A *twin* sister."

"A TWIN? And they separated them?"

"I'm afraid so. She was sent to the preserve in Kenya when he was sent to the Bio-allmeans Laboratory."

"Why?"

"She was to be the 'control' part of Bucky's experiment."

"That's terrible. The whole idea of Friday being part of an . . . an 'experiment' is terrible." She patted her lap, and Friday loped over and climbed onto it. She kissed his nose. How could anyone do that to an animal for the sake of a better banana?

"Bucky's last trip was to enlist Dee Dee's help in getting Merga—Friday—out of the country and to the preserve before he was too humanly imprinted and where he would be safe."

"Well, he's safe here," Rachel said.

Her father's eyes looked sad. "Is he?"

As she undressed for bed, Rachel didn't want to think about what she was thinking about, but she couldn't help

Hester Mundis

it. Friday was sitting cross-legged on the floor and gazing at photographs of chimpanzees in her *National Geographic* magazine. The thought that he might be looking for his twin sister tore at her heart.

She felt the start of a tear in the corner of her eye. She loved Friday more than she'd allowed herself to love anyone or anything since her mother had died. He'd come into her life and filled up that empty place. She couldn't bear to think of parting with him. No, that was unthinkable. Who in the jungle would give him the cream cheese and jelly sandwiches he had come to love? Who would kiss him good night and tickle his feet?

Surely, in New York City, in an apartment with three locks on the door and friendly pizza deliverymen and the best medical center for animals nearby, he'd be better off than anywhere else in the world. Wouldn't he?

Friday's lips were pressed to the page of the magazine.

Rachel threw herself down on her bed and cried.

Friday tilted his head toward her and climbed onto the bed. He hooted softly and pushed his face next to hers. He looked confused. He looked concerned. He looked lonely.

Rachel sobbed uncontrollably.

The next morning, Rachel called Brianne to tell her about Bucky Greene's coat, but she wasn't home. Her stepfather said that her mother had taken her to her father's house in New Jersey because it was her stepsister's birthday. So much for Brianne's saying she never went where she didn't want to go. She hated her stepsister Valerie with a vengeance. Valerie was always making fun of Brianne's height, saying, "How's the weather up there," and calling her names like "flagpole"; "giraffasaurus"; and the "walking tower of pizza." To get even, Brianne once put soap in her milk, and Valerie threw up all over her piano teacher and the piano. Then their cat licked the keys and threw up in Valerie's slipper. Brianne said it smelled awful, but it was worth being there to see.

When Rachel called Mickey, he came right over. "What's the matter with your eyes?" he asked.

"I—I got soap in them this morning." She wasn't about to tell Mickey Phelps that she had cried all night. He'd ask why, and she'd probably tell him and then she might start crying again.

"Is that it?" he asked, pointing to Bucky Greene's coat.

"That's it."

"That is ug-a-ly!"

"You're telling me."

"A computer in a coat, huh." He shook his head, bending down to look at it.

"It's more than just the computer." Rachel showed him all the pockets. "It's a file cabinet in a coat." She waved her arm toward the stack of papers in the corner. "That's just some of what was in there."

"There was more?"

"We threw away the gum wrappers and banana peels."

"Banana peels? He carried around banana peels?"

"It was his job. He took work home."

"He was a Frankenfood maker?"

"He was just trying to—to build a better banana." Rachel didn't know why she was defending Bucky Greene. She was opposed to genetically altered foods as Mickey was. But Bucky had cared about Friday enough to want to protect him, and that was worth defending him for. She turned her head toward Friday and smiled.

The chimp had hoisted himself in the Upmobile to the top of her bookcase and was happily eating a cream cheese and jelly sandwich. Wetspot lay on the floor below, keeping an eye open for any cream cheese fallout.

Mickey looked at the computer. "Does it work?"

"Ah . . . no," she said quickly, averting her eyes. Mickey had a way of knowing just by looking at her when she was lying. Sometimes he didn't even have to look at her. This was one of those times.

"It does work, doesn't it?" He poked her in the shoulder. "Come on, let me see."

Her father had told her that until he found out more from Dee Dee VanAusdale about Bucky's trip to Kenya, the fewer people who knew about the Nana Banana Chronicles the safer for all concerned. "Okay, it works. But I'm not supposed to turn it on."

Mickey raised an eyebrow. "Since when do you not do what you're not supposed to?"

"What's that supposed to mean?"

"It's not *supposed* to mean something. It means exactly what I said. You weren't supposed to take Friday anywhere without asking your dad—and you did. You weren't supposed to tell Brianne what Karla said about her, but you did. You weren't supposed to—"

"All right. You win . . . I suppose," she added grudgingly.

"Come on. Show me."

"Okay." Why not? Her father was just being overly cautious. If she could be overly suspicious, he could be overly cautious. Besides, Mickey was going to be so impressed—and impressing Mickey Phelps was like winning a game.

My Chimp Friday

She connected the wires, and the screen lit up.

"Wow." Mickey's eyes widened. "That is too cool."

"You want to see something even cooler than that?"

"Sure."

Rachel waved. "Friday. Come on down."

Friday hooted and pitched the last of his cream cheese and jelly sandwich to Wetspot, who caught it with no difficulty, and slid down the rope.

Rachel tilted her chin toward the coat. "Go ahead. What's the password?"

Friday leaned over the computer keyboard.

"You're not telling me—"

"Shhh."

Mickey watched openmouthed as Friday typed the word "BANANA." Bucky's list of classified files appeared on the screen; "the Nana Banana Chronicles" highlighted in yellow.

"This looks big-time."

"It is."

"What's it all about?"

Rachel hesitated. If she told him about the nana banana formula in Friday's DNA, he might know too much and be in danger. If she didn't tell him, he might not know enough to know that he might be in danger. It was all very confusing. The safest thing to do was to tell him everything. So she did.

Less than an hour later she regretted every word of it.

Hester Mundis

17.

Déjà Danger

Where are we taking this thing?" Mickey asked as he and Rachel half carried, half dragged Bucky's coat to the elevator.

"To our storage bay in the basement." Rachel turned around. "Jared? Do you have the keys?"

Jared jingled them. "Yep. And here comes the elevator."

The door opened, and Mickey and Rachel yanked the coat in with them. As the elevator started down, the coat jiggled. Then it hooted.

"I don't believe it." Rachel put her hands on her hips. Friday had squeezed himself into the pocket where they had removed the computer. "You little devil. How did you get in there?"

Friday's shoulders moved up and down as if he were laughing.

"Should we go back up?" Mickey asked

"It'll be all right. He can come with us. Jared, you can hold him. We won't be long."

The elevator opened onto the basement. The bulb in

the main room had gone out, and it was darker than usual. Rachel had that funny feeling at the back of her neck and she didn't like it. Why did people always call them "funny feelings" when there was nothing funny about them? She looked around for Mr. Aplox, but neither he nor Attila were there.

"It's creepy down here," Jared said.

Friday agreed with a drawn-out spooky "hoo-hoo."

"We're just going over there." She pointed to the storage area, which was farther away than she'd remembered.

"There's not a lot of light there." Only two small windows at the far corner were visible.

"Jared!" she said impatiently, because she didn't like it down there any more than he did and that funny feeling that wasn't really funny wasn't going away. "We're not going to read a book. We're just going to throw the coat in with your sled and dad's skis. Come on."

Their storage bay was number 6. A stout wooden door with a latch and handle arrangement instead of a knob enclosed it. Rachel unlocked the latch. "Okay, let's—"

There were footsteps. Voices. "They're down here somewhere. I saw them in the elevator."

Rachel, Jared, and Mickey froze.

"You go that way. I'll go this way. We'll get him this time."

Him! Him had to be Friday. Rachel's heart began to pound like a jackhammer in her chest.

"What about the kids?"

"You have a gun. Do whatever you have to do," the voice yelled angrily. "Just get that chimp!"

"It's the chimp-napp—" Rachel put her hand over Jared's mouth.

Hester Mundis

"Over there!" the voice shouted.

They were getting closer.

"Quick," Rachel whispered. "We've got to hide."

"Where?"

There was only one thing that could conceal all of them. Rachel pointed, and they dove under the coat, which enveloped them in frightening total blackness.

Friday screeched and pulled away, leaping to the pipes above and swinging hand over hand across the ceiling of the basement.

Rachel started to call him back, but Mickey clapped his hand over her mouth. "You want to get us killed?" he whispered fiercely.

Rachel shook her head and listened.

"Hey, look up there," a voice nearby shouted. "I think that's him."

"Where?"

"It was just there a minute ago. Damn!" There was the sound of a chair falling over. "If those kids are down here, we'd better make sure they stay down here. If you know what I mean."

Rachel knew what they meant. She put her arm around Jared and held her breath. She prayed that Friday would find a hiding place before they found him. She prayed that their hiding place wouldn't be found. She prayed that what was happening wasn't really happening. And if it was happening, that something would happen to make it stop happening.

"There he is! Get him!" There was the sound of a scuffle. "Damn it! He got away again."

Just then Friday began to screech and screech and screech. Rachel's heart sank. They've got him!

My Chimp Friday 127

BANG! A gunshot echoed in the basement.

Ohmygod, they've killed him! Rachel thought. She was too terrified to cry.

"That was dumb!" The voice was angry. "Let's hurry this up."

"What the—" Mr. Aplox's words were cut off by Attila's bone-chilling growl, followed by vicious snarling and barking.

Sounds seemed to bounce off the walls of the basement. Rachel couldn't tell where they were coming from. More barking. Cursing. The clang of metal. The thud of something falling. A body?

Then there was silence. Attila had stopped barking. Was he dead, too?

Footsteps were coming toward the storage area. Rachel squeezed her eyes shut as she, Jared, and Mickey gripped one another's hands. Please don't let them find us.

The footsteps stopped. Someone was close by. Rachel's heart was pounding so hard she thought her chest would shatter.

Slowly the coat concealing them was being pulled back.

Was this it? Was this . . . 'curtains'? Rachel unsqueezed her eyes slowly. She blinked, and then suddenly breathed, "Thank God."

"Thank God . . . what?" Jared asked, his voice quavering, eyes still shut.

"Thank God . . . it's Friday!" She felt as if she would collapse with relief. Friday tugged her arm and began to hoot loudly.

"I think he wants us to get out of here."

"He's not the only one," Mickey said. "Come on. We've got to get the police."

   Hester Mundis

"Are you kids all right?" It was Mr. Aplox. The footsteps had been his.

"For now. But those men"—Rachel looked around quickly—"are they still here? They want my chimp. They have a gun and—"

"Had a gun," Mr. Aplox said, holding the pistol. "When Attila lunged, the guy dropped it . . . and Attila wasn't about to let him reach for it. Were you, boy?"

The terror of West Eighty-seventh Street padded over from across the room, looking quite pleased with himself. Rachel would never let anyone say a bad word about Attila again.

Mr. Aplox thumped the dog's hindquarters proudly. "They took off real fast after that."

"But they might come back," Jared said, glancing around. "Or, maybe they're still here."

"He's right," Mickey said.

"We're not staying to find out." Rachel grabbed her brother's shoulders. "Jared, you take Friday upstairs in the elevator right now. Mickey and I will go find Dad. He's at the grocery."

Mr. Aplox said that he and Attila would take another look around.

Mickey and Rachel ran up the alley stairs. Rachel froze when she looked across the street. Pickle Nose was there, and he was staring up at their building. He had to be casing it for some reason, and Rachel had a pretty good idea that the reason was in the elevator on the way up to her apartment.

"Mickey," she said through clenched teeth, "don't look now, but that guy across the street is the one I've been telling you about. You know, the one who's been hanging around here every day? I think he might be one of *them*."

"Let's put a move on it, then," Mickey said.

"Let's." Rachel turned and saw Wendy Mills coming toward them.

"My goodness, Rachel. You look upset."

"The chimp-nappers are back. One had a gun, and—"

"Did they get your chimp?"

"No, but I'm afraid they will."

"Where is he now? Is there anything I can do?"

"Well . . . yes. You could stay with him and my brother Jared until we get back."

"Of course."

"It's apartment 3D. We're going to get my dad. Tell Jared who you are, and that I told you to stay with him, and make sure he doesn't let any strangers in."

"You have my word on it."

Rachel felt better knowing that Jared wouldn't be alone while they were gone. But the feeling didn't last long. Coming around the corner at that moment was Aunt Lisa accompanied by a young blond woman in blue jeans who was carrying a cake box. "Rachel," Aunt Lisa said, smiling, "we were just coming to—"

"Can't talk now."

"Excuse me?" Aunt Lisa's smile was history. "And what, may I ask, is this big hurry that you haven't time to kiss your aunt who's been away for eight days"—she made it sound as if she'd been in jail for eight years—"and to say a polite hello to my friend Wendy Mills?"

"Aunt Lisa, we're—what? WENDY MILLS? You mean, she . . . her . . . this is your friend Wendy Mills?"

"Why, yes," Aunt Lisa said, confused.

"I brought you a cake," said Wendy Mills.

"But then who . . . ?" Rachel's voice trailed off.

"It's an upside-down cake," Wendy Mills said cheerily.

"Oh, no!" Rachel cried, her face turning as gray as the cake box. "Upside down! That's it!"

"You don't like upside-down cake?"

Suddenly Rachel realized why the woman she thought was Wendy Mills wasn't Wendy Mills at all. The initials that she'd seen on her bracelet had been upside down. They weren't a **W** and an **M.** They were an **M** and a **W.** An **M** and a **W** as in Mimi Wykaire. The same Mimi Wykaire, who Bucky Greene had warned them about, who would stop at nothing to get what she wanted.

And at that very moment, what Mimi Wykaire wanted was upstairs with Jared—and now so was she!

18.

Rescue Rampage

We've got to stop her!" Rachel screamed, grabbing Mickey's arm and heading back into the building.

"Stop who?" Aunt Lisa called, hurrying after them, the real Wendy Mills trailing behind, still holding the cake.

"Find Mr. Aplox! Call the police!" Rachel shouted. "We can't let her get away. She'll do anything to get that chimp."

"Chimp? Chimpanzee?" Aunt Lisa looked totally flummoxed. "What chimpanzee? Whose chimpanzee?"

"Our chimpanzee," Rachel said. "Hurry. Jared could be in danger."

"Since when do you have a chimpanzee?" Aunt Lisa was now running alongside them. The real Wendy Mills followed, looking totally lost, her cake box jiggling precariously.

"MR. APLOX! HELP!" Rachel shouted when she caught sight of him. "Bring Attila with you. They're going to get our chimp. We've got to stop her. She's in our apartment now."

Mr. Aplox and Attila bounded across the lobby. Aunt Lisa and her friend froze. "He's fine," Mr. Aplox said quickly. "Just don't make any sudden moves." He turned to Rachel. "Now who's this 'her'?"

"That lady I thought was my aunt's friend who was after my father wasn't my aunt's friend after all. All she's after is my chimp." The words spewed like celery from a SaladShooter.

"There's a real chimpanzee in the apartment?" Aunt Lisa's face contorted in a strange way.

"There won't be if we don't stop her," Rachel wailed. "We can't let her get away."

"We won't," Mr. Aplox said, patting Attila significantly. "You"—he nodded to Mickey—"stall the elevator. We'll take the stairs."

"What's going on here?"

"DADDY!" Rachel ran to her father. "Friday's going to be chimp-napped. We have to hurry." Rachel tugged his sleeve. "And Jared could be in danger."

"Jared."

"Ben, what's this about a chimp?"

Her father looked as if he just been spun through a revolving door. "Oh, Lisa. You're back."

"This is my friend—"

"Not now, Aunt Lisa." Rachel grabbed her father's hand. "DADDY, NOW!"

"Wait a minute, honey—"

"We CAN'T wait." This was certainly no time for his saintly patience.

"She's right," Mr. Aplox said. Then he shouted something in German, and Attila lurched for the staircase.

Rachel and her father took off right behind them, followed by Aunt Lisa, who was repeatedly mumbling "a chimpanzee?" and the real Wendy Mills, who was now clutching the cake box like a life preserver.

The door to the apartment was slightly open. When she

My Chimp Friday

saw it, Rachel's heart began to pound so fast, she was almost unable to breathe. Were they too late?

With Attila barking at rottweiler rage level, Mr. Aplox hurtled into the apartment.

What happened next was something that none of them would ever forget. It was also something they had trouble believing they were seeing. Even Attila stopped barking and stared.

At the end of the hall, legs and arms splayed in different directions, Mimi Wykaire lay on the floor, thoroughly soaked from head to toe in root beer. Her dark hair drooped over her face like strings of inky seaweed. Root beer ran down her forehead and off her nose. Everything she wore was dripping, and she was sputtering.

Wetspot stood four paws square opposite her—growling. Really *growling*. Rachel had never heard Wetspot growl before. Nobody had. It was extremely impressive. But what was more impressive was that he was holding his ground and growling with Friday sitting astride him—hooting nonstop—and waving a real pistol like a cartoon cowboy in front of Mimi Wykaire's enraged, root beer-blurred face.

"It worked. My booby trap worked!" Jared shouted. "She never knew what hit her."

"She knows now," Rachel said. The apartment reeked of sarsparilla.

"Why, you stupid little—" Mimi Wykaire attempted to get to her feet, but Wetspot and Attila lunged forward with a growl duet that sent her back on her butt.

"I'm not stupid and I'm not little," Rachel said. "But you're a creep and a loser."

"You actually have a real chimpanzee," Aunt Lisa said, shaking her head and staring at Friday.

"And he's holding a real gun," Jared pointed out.

"I'd better take that, Friday." Rachel's father took the pistol and Friday dismounted and darted to Rachel, who picked him up and kissed him.

"Ben! I can't believe you let a dirty animal like that in your house."

"She wasn't invited." Rachel's father smiled at Mimi Wykaire, who sneered.

"I mean the chimp."

"He's not dirty," Rachel said.

"It's a chimpanzee. They spit, they bite, they . . . they play with themselves."

"He doesn't spit, he doesn't bite, and he has toys," Rachel's father said gently, exhibiting his saintly patience at its saintliest. Rachel was personally ready to haul off and whack her aunt.

"Would anyone like a piece of upside-down cake?" Wendy Mills asked meekly.

What a ditz, Rachel thought, and immediately felt guilty for thinking it. Ditz or not, the truth was, she had saved Friday. If Aunt Lisa hadn't brought her over today, they might not have known that the fake Wendy Mills was really Mimi Wykaire until it was too late. They might have lost Friday forever.

"I'd better call the police before that sicko's pals come looking for her." Mr. Aplox started for the phone.

"Hold it right there. I'll take it from here," a voice said.

Rachel gasped.

Standing in the doorway, holding a gun in one hand and Mickey's arm in the other, was Pickle Nose.

My Chimp Friday

19.

When Good Guys Are Bad

Everyone in the room froze. Rachel's stomach did a sickening somersault as she turned to see if Mimi Wykaire was going for a *who's-laughing-now* laugh before she shot her for being nasty, but M. W. looked as stunned as the rest of them. She didn't know who Pickle Nose was either.

Attila growled. Mr. Aplox had a German command on the tip of his tongue and was about to utter it when Pickle Nose pulled open his jacket and flashed a badge. "Eric Wilens, FBI."

FBI? *The* FBI? Rachel couldn't believe it. A federal agent right there in their apartment! Wait until she told Brianne. She tried to catch Mickey's eye to see if he was as impressed as she was, but he looked kind of like he'd just gotten off a roller coaster after eating a hot-fudge sundae with a chili dog.

"We've been after this slippery eel"—he nodded toward Mimi Wykaire—"for some time. The agency has been trolling for her and her walleyed husband ever since we were tipped off that they were involved in some dirty international angling involving stolen DNA. Their whole Bio-allmeans operation smelt . . . er, smelled fishy, but we had no real evidence against them, and the case was floundering. They kept slipping through our net. I was determined to reel them in, and you supplied the perfect bait."

He was making it sound as if FBI stood for Fishing Bureau of Investigation.

"Her shrimpy little husband and the other bottom-feeder with him who tried to grab the chimp in the basement are on their way to Davey Jones's lockup already."

Agent Wilens definitely had a thing for the sea. Rachel pegged him for a Pisces.

"It's a lucky fluke that we were finally able to tie them to a few 'accidents' that were actually 'on porpoise'—er, on purpose."

"By 'on purpose,' you mean . . ." Her father's voice trailed off significantly.

Agent Wilens nodded. "M-u-r-d-e-r."

"Murder!" Aunt Lisa exclaimed. "I'm away from this family for eight days and you're involved with the FBI, killers, kidnappers, chimpanzees. It's a good thing I didn't go for the resort's two-week package."

"Was one of those 'accidents' Bucky Greene?" Rachel asked.

Agent Wilens nodded again. "Making murder look like accidents is what these sharks have been doing for quite a while. Greene slipping on a banana peel wasn't the first one down the pike. No, these Bio-allmeans barracudas are as cold-blooded as they come."

"All right already with the fish stuff," Aunt Lisa exploded. She wasn't one to hold back. "Arrest her. We've got a lot of cleaning to do here."

Agent Wilens grabbed Mimi Wykaire's wrist and

jerked her to her feet. "Come on, you're going into the tank for a long time."

Mimi Wykaire spat two words at him. They were definitely not among Mr. DeFina's enriching ones. Rachel's father coughed, and Aunt Lisa looked at the ceiling.

"Bucky Greene was a fool," Mimi Wykaire said angrily. "He could have been rich if he'd played ball with us. But no, your friend Greene was too moral for that." She sneered at Ben as she spoke. A smile curled her lips evilly. "We thought it was fitting to give him the final slip—with his own banana peel."

Friday reached out suddenly from Rachel's arms and yanked Mimi Wykaire's hair hard.

"Ow! You dirty little ba—"

Friday screeched and would have pulled her hair again if Rachel hadn't stopped him. Not that she wanted to stop him. She knew how much he must have loved Bucky Greene. She also knew he had understood everything that had just been said, but she knew better than to say anything about that. As far as she was concerned, he could have pulled out every hair on Mimi Wykaire's head. But she didn't want him to fuel Aunt Lisa's ape hostility further. She was going to have to figure out a way Friday could really suck up to her.

Agent Wilens snapped a pair of handcuffs on Mimi Wykaire and smiled broadly, making his pickle nose look even more like a gherkin. Then, to Rachel's horror, he lifted his sleeve up to it. Oh, no! How could an FBI agent do that? And in public! She grabbed a tissue and wondered how embarrassing it would be if she threw it at him. Would it be more embarrassing if she didn't? Before she could decide, she saw that she didn't have to. Agent Wilens was

Hester Mundis

talking to his sleeve. Talking! There was a phone-radio inside his jacket! He hadn't been wiping his nose on his clothes after all! He'd been keeping in contact with other agents. That certainly made her feel a lot better about the FBI in general—and Agent Wilens in particular.

A short while later, two men entered the apartment. They wore jackets emblazoned with the letters FBI, leaving no doubt as to who they were or why they were doing what they were doing, which at that moment was unceremoniously leading Mimi Wykaire away.

Rachel swung Friday between her legs and then back up into her arms. "No more chimp-nappers! Now I don't have to worry about you being taken away from me ever, ever, ever."

Friday hooted and clapped his hands.

"This calls for a banana," Jared said. "And I happen to have one." He handed it to Friday, who scrambled down onto the couch to eat it.

Rachel's father thanked Agent Wilens and shook his hand. Rachel thanked him, too. He told them not to mention it and that it was he who should be thanking them, because the Wykaires were a "real catch." (Rachel ignored his use of the phrase.) Then he just stood there looking as if he had forgotten what he was going to say or didn't know how to say whatever it was in the first place.

There was an awkward silence. Wendy Mills asked again if anyone wanted cake. No one answered, not even Jared, who had an automatic "yes" for anything that came from a bakery. All eyes were focused on Agent Wilens, who was definitely about to say . . . *something*. What on earth was he waiting for?

"Er—yes?" Rachel's father said encouragingly. "Is there something else?"

My Chimp Friday

Agent Wilens was looking at Friday eating the banana. He was looking at him in a way that gave Rachel that unfunny funny feeling on the back of her neck.

"Mr. Stelson"—Agent Wilens looked uncomfortable—"the government has reason to believe that this chimp from the Bio-allmeans Lab may be holding the key to an important genetic breakthrough in intelligence."

"I wouldn't be a bit"—Mickey caught himself—"uh, *sure* of that. He's pretty . . . ordinary."

"Very," Rachel said. "Very ordinary."

"He can't even beat me at chess," chimed Jared, suddenly realizing it was the wrong thing to say. Rachel glared at her brother, who quickly stammered, "And I'm a really bad player."

"I'm a science professor," Rachel's father said, looking very professorial, "and if you ask me, he is a pretty average chimpanzee."

Agent Wilens stared at the floor as if he didn't want to say what he was going to say any more than they wanted to hear it. But he said it, anyway. "I'm sorry, but the government has authorized me to commandeer him for examination at their primate testing lab."

"NO!" Rachel cried. She felt tears filling her eyes. "You can't take him away. He hasn't done anything. He's not yours." She ran to her father. "Daddy, don't let him take him to that laboratory. Please. Please."

"Rachel, control yourself," Aunt Lisa said. "It's just a chimpanzee."

If ever Rachel wanted to strangle her aunt, it was then.

"Lisa! That's enough." Rachel's father's voice was stern. Aunt Lisa turned her head and huffed. "Now, honey"—he stroked Rachel's hair—"just take it easy for a moment."

Hester Mundis

"I'm sorry." Agent Wilens made a gesture of helplessness. "It's my job. The government can't ignore information of this magnitude if it could be true. They need to run a series of IQ tests on him. If the tests show nothing remarkable, you'll have him back in a matter of a few hours."

"But what if he seems. . . er, really intelligent? What then?"

"I'm afraid I don't know." Agent Wilens averted his eyes.

He knows all right! He's afraid to say what he knows, Rachel thought. He's afraid to say that they'll do whatever they need to do to find out what makes Friday tick. They'll turn him into an experiment. "Daddy, we can't let them take Friday."

Rachel's father held his hand up. "Of course, we want to cooperate with the government."

"No, we don't!" Rachel cried. How could he have said that?

"Where is this primate testing lab?"

"It's in Clifton, New Jersey. Why?"

"Give me the address and let us take him there. We'll do it tomorrow. It will be much less stressful for . . . for the chimp."

Agent Wilens scratched his head. "I don't know."

"I do. I'm a professor." Rachel had never heard her father use his job as a credential before. "Stress can alter test results. It'll be better for you if we take him there."

Agent Wilens looked at Rachel, then at Jared. "I've got two kids at home. I know how they'd feel if a stranger was going to take their dog away. Okay." He took a card from his pocket. "Have him here at ten o'clock tomorrow morning."

My Chimp Friday

"You have my word."

"I'll meet you there," said Agent Wilens, and he left.

No one spoke. The apartment was so quiet, you could have heard a jaw drop.

"Cake, anyone?" asked Wendy Mills.

The ride to New Jersey the following morning was gloomy. Friday sensed that something was wrong. Rachel handed him the Rubik's Cube and when he solved it and handed it back, she turned away so he couldn't see her eyes. "Why do you have to be so smart," she said angrily.

Friday climbed in her lap and pushed his face close to hers as if trying to comprehend what she'd said. He "hoo-hoo'd" quizzically.

"Couldn't you just be an average vine-swinging ape? You know, the kind that wouldn't get upset if you didn't let him watch music videos on TV?" Two nights before, he had thrown a top-of-the-charts-thirty-two-distinct-sound tantrum when Rachel had wanted to watch something other than MTV.

Friday scratched his head.

She wished there had never been a "nana banana." She wished they were driving in any other direction than toward the primate lab in Clifton, New Jersey. She rubbed the Rubik's Cube and wished it really was a lucky charm.

"How much farther?"

"We're almost there." Her father usually whistled when they drove somewhere. He hadn't let out a peep since they'd left.

Friday rummaged through the bag of treats Rachel had brought. He took out a box of raisins and began tossing them in the air and catching them in his mouth. No one said a word. The silence in the car was deafening.

They went through the gate at the Clifton Laboratory for Primate Research and drove up to a small booth where a guard checked a clipboard for their name and then waved them through.

Agent Wilens met them at the delivery entrance. Standing beside him were two white-coated laboratory assistants. Next to them was an empty steel mesh cage on wheels.

Friday saw it and stiffened in Rachel's arms. He began to "hoot" noisily.

As one of the lab assistants reached for him, his fur bristled like a porcupine and he started to screech-bark furiously. "Uh-UH-Oh-Uh-UH-oh-Uh-ee-EE-ee-OH!" It sounded like "Old MacDonald Had a Farm" sung by someone whose finger was caught in a car door. (Jared called it "The Broken Power Drill," number twenty-seven of Friday's distinct thirty-two.)

"He doesn't need to be in a cage," Rachel explained. "He's very well behaved." At which moment Friday spit right in the lab assistant's face.

Rachel was stunned. "I—I'm so sorry. He's never done that before."

"We're used to it. Lots of them do it." He put Friday in the cage and closed it quickly. Friday studied the latch. Rachel's eyes widened, and she gave a barely perceptible shake to her head. All she needed was for him to show off his Houdini skills.

As they wheeled him inside the building, Friday clung to the bars of the little cage like a condemned prisoner. "It'll be all right," Rachel called. She hoped he believed her. She wished that she believed herself.

My Chimp Friday

"You can wait in the reception area," Agent Wilens said, "but it might be a while. There's a coffee shop two blocks over. You could have lunch."

Rachel's father thanked him and said they would do that. None of them were hungry, but sitting in a coffee shop looking at a sandwich and fries was better than sitting in a laboratory where they were doing who-knew-what to Friday. And whatever they were doing, Rachel didn't want to think about.

When they returned three hours later they were told that "the subject was still under observation."

Rachel plopped gloomily down on the leather bench in the waiting room. Friday wasn't a "subject"! Math was a subject. English was a subject. Friday was a . . . a person. Maybe not a human person, but he was a person nonetheless. And she didn't care if that was s-p-e-c-i-o-u-s reasoning. "I wish I knew what they were looking for," Rachel grumbled.

"Whatever it is, honey, we can only hope that they don't find it."

After what seemed like an eternity but was actually only fifteen more minutes, Agent Wilens emerged from a door at the end of the corridor and marched toward them. Next to him was an orderly wheeling Friday in a cage. As they approached, Rachel's heart flip-flopped in her chest. She tried to read their faces, but they were expressionless.

Agent Wilens halted directly in front of where they were sitting. So close that neither Rachel nor her father could stand up. Rachel stared at the cage. Friday didn't look up. He didn't look down, either. He looked . . . bored. He was lying on his back examining his fingers and toes as if he'd never seen them before. What had they done to him?

Hester Mundis

Agent Wilens cleared his throat. "I have some good news and some bad news for you."

Good news, bad news? This wasn't a joke! Rachel gripped her father's arm. Jared gripped hers. Sitting together on that bench, they looked as if they were about to go on a scary ride—or were they already on it?

"What's the good news?" Her father always tried to look on the bright side first. Rachel would have wanted to know the worst and gotten it over with.

"Well, it's really just *sort* of good news. You see, they gave him all the standard primate intelligence tests and . . ." His voice trailed off, and he looked very somber for someone about to deliver any sort of *good* news.

"And?"

"And the information we received about him being the link to a DNA breakthrough in engineered intelligence turned out to be false. He showed absolutely no signs of possessing any special genetic gifts." Agent Wilens grinned broadly.

"You mean . . . ?" Rachel held her breath. She wasn't taking anything for granted. The FBI worked in mysterious ways. Agent Wilens could have given them a trick answer.

"You heard me. The government has no use for him. He's yours."

"Yes!" Rachel screamed. "Yes, yes, YES!"

"Whoopie!" Jared shouted, immediately jumping up and nearly knocking out one of Agent Wilens's teeth with his head.

"Now, kids, let's just—"

"Did you hear that, Daddy? He's ours."

"Yes, yes. But—"

My Chimp Friday

"No buts about it. He's ours." The orderly opened the cage, and Rachel scooped Friday into her arms, smothering him with kisses. Jared handed him a box of raisins.

"Okay," her father said, facing Agent Wilens, who was still rubbing his jaw, "you said there was good news and bad news. I think that before this"—he indicated Rachel's and Jared's excitement—"goes too far . . . you'd better give us the bad news."

"Are you sure you want to hear it?"

Rachel wasn't sure that she did, but her father nodded, so she had no choice. In a way, she was glad. She hated making decisions. Agent Wilens hesitated and stared at the cuff of his shirt. For goodness' sake, was he planning to deliver the Gettysburg address?

"All right. You asked for it." It sounded like he was about to punch her father in the nose. "The bad news is that your chimp over there"—he pointed as if they had another one somewhere else—"is reading off an empty disk."

"Huh?"

"The cheese has slid off his cracker."

"I beg your pardon?"

"He's a few clowns short of a circus. You know, the wheel is spinning, but the hamster's dead."

"I'm afraid I—"

"His Slinky's kinked!"

"What are you saying?"

"I am saying," Agent Wilens said, loudly and with no small amount of annoyance, "that your ape doesn't even know the difference between *you* and *me!*"

"You and me? What do we—"

"Not you and me," Agent Wilens snapped. "Just *you* and *me.*"

Hester Mundis

"Us?"

Agent Wilens exploded. "Listen to me! I'm telling you that your chimpanzee is not only NOT overly intelligent, but as far as chimpanzees go in the world of chimpanzees—and they can go quite far—he is definitely NOT the brightest banana in the bunch!"

Talk about accentuating the negative!

"Oh," said her father. And they left.

20.

A Stupid Mistake

Rachel didn't get it and said so. "I don't get it. I mean, I'm happy that they didn't find out how intelligent Friday is, but why didn't they?"

"I'm mystified myself," her father confessed.

"Agent Wilens made it sound like Friday had the brains of a bobby pin." She looked down at him, and her brow furrowed. He had been playing with the Rubik's Cube since they'd left the laboratory, but it was like he'd never seen it before. "Go on, you can do it."

Friday looked at her blankly.

"Solve the puzzle. Make this side all yellow." She pointed to the color. Friday dropped the Cube and tugged at her hair. "Hey, cut that out."

He pushed his lips out into a pout and launched into a string of noisy "HOO-HOO-HOO-HOOs!"

"Come on, Friday." Rachel held out the Cube, but he ignored it. Instead, he picked up a box of raisins and began examining it. To her amazement, he looked puzzled about how to open it. What had they done to him? Had they given him some sort of stupid pill? "Daddy, Friday's not . . . himself. He's not doing the Rubik's Cube and he doesn't seem to understand what I'm saying."

"Are we sure that's Friday?" Jared asked cautiously.

"That's the dumbest question I've ever heard," Rachel snapped. Actually it wasn't the dumbest question she'd *ever* heard. Last month when she was dragging a ladder into her bedroom, Aunt Lisa had asked her if she wanted to fall down and break every bone in her body. Now *that* was the dumbest question she'd ever heard. "Of course it's Friday. Look at him. He's wearing the little New York Yankees T-shirt Brianne gave him."

"They could have put that on another chimp and taken the real Friday away for more experiments," Jared said quickly, as if he were on to something. "They do that in Bond movies all the time."

"They don't have chimps in Bond movies," Rachel said making a face at him.

"They do it with PEOPLE! In—I think it was *You Only Live Twice*—they did it with James Bond himself!"

"Jared, they didn't switch chimps," Rachel said, slamming her hand on the seat for emphasis and scaring Friday from her lap. "He's the same chimp we brought there this morning."

"Oh, yeah? Are you sure?" Friday was rocking back and forth and sucking his finger.

"I'm sure!" she shouted. (She was sure. Wasn't she?) Oh, sure, she knew she was often sure about a lot of things that she shouldn't have been sure about, but Friday wasn't one of them. This chimp was definitely Friday. No doubt about it. But he sure wasn't the same chimp they'd brought in that morning. Only five hours earlier he had been buckling and unbuckling the seat belt in the back. At the moment, all he was doing was chewing on it.

"Maybe they shrunk his brain with something?"

"Jared, that is ridiculous," Rachel said, and her father agreed.

"I agree," he said, "but he's certainly a changed chimp."

There was no denying that! From a simian Einstein to a furry dumbbell in less than a day. Rachel wondered if he could be in shock. She'd read that people who were "in shock" forgot things. Sometimes they couldn't talk or didn't remember who they were or where they were or how to hold a fork or even use a toothbrush. She asked her father if he thought that was a possibility, but he doubted it seriously.

"I seriously doubt it."

"There's got to be SOME reason for his turning stupid." She was angry and didn't know at whom she was angry. It wasn't that she would stop loving him if he did turn into an ordinary ape, but it wasn't fair. He was probably the smartest chimp in the whole world. The side effects from Bucky Greene's genetically engineered nana banana had made him that, but—wait a minute, maybe that was it! That had to be it. She was sure of it. "Daddy. I know what's happened to Friday."

"You do?"

"He's turned into a jerk," Jared said. "Look." Friday was trying to put a cap back onto a ballpoint pen with no success.

"It's wearing off!"

"What's wearing off?"

"The side effects from the nana banana. Sure, they were good side effects and they made him smarter, but they were side effects, and side effects can wear off, can't they?"

"Sometimes. It depends on the organism, the genes involved, age, health, weather, new foods—"

"Just about anything, right?"

"Theoretically, yes. It is conceivable that the nana banana syndrome may have run its course."

"Well, that's it, then."

"What's it?" Jared asked, annoyed.

"The nana banana side effects that made him intelligent have worn off, and he's just a regular chimpanzee." She smoothed Friday's hair gently.

"An irregular chimpanzee, if you ask me." Friday was still struggling to fit the cap onto the pen.

"I don't care if he is the dumbest animal in the whole world," Rachel said stubbornly, even though she feared that she sort of did care—but if she did, she wasn't going to admit it to herself. "I love him just because he's who he is. And he's wonderful." She kissed his head. "I love you, Friday."

He dropped the pen. Putting his fingers on her cheek, he stroked her face and "hoo-hoo'd" softly. Then suddenly he grabbed the Rubik's Cube and, before they reached the next traffic light, he'd solved the puzzle.

"I don't believe it!" Rachel squealed. "Look, Daddy. Look!"

"I'm driving, honey. I need to watch the road. What is it?"

"He solved the puzzle!"

"In record time, too."

Friday "hoot-hooted" joyfully and waved the Cube in

the air. Then he mixed the puzzle up and did it again.

"Not the brightest banana in the bunch? Ha!" Her father slapped the steering wheel.

"'Ha!' is right," Rachel said triumphantly. "He's a genuine chimpanzee genius, aren't you?" Friday's head bobbed. "He's so smart, he was able to fool the Federal Bureau of Investigation! It takes a really, really smart chimpanzee to know when to play dumb."

"Why was he playing dumb with us?" Jared asked. "We're not the FBI."

"I know we're not the FBI! I'm sure it was just to be certain that we were okay to be trusted again. After all, we did take him out there."

"You were *sure* his side effects were wearing off just ten minutes ago, too," Jared pointed out.

"All right, then," Rachel said, annoyed at being caught at being *sure* again, "he did it because . . . because . . . because he had his reasons. OKAY?"

Jared put his hands up in mock self-defense. "Okay, okay. Don't make a federal case out of it."

"I don't have to. Friday already did that!"

Ben Stelson beeped the horn. The car ahead of them had a bumper sticker that said, HONK IF YOU'RE HAPPY. It had also just switched lanes without signaling. Rachel didn't care which had prompted her father to honk. It was a celebratory noise, like the kind you make on New Year's Eve, and she had never had more reason to celebrate. If happiness was on a scale of one to ten, she was at eleven. From now on, Friday would be safe and smart and could stay with her forever.

21.

Out of Africa

The letter arrived the following Saturday. Rachel had just come back from the park where she and Brianne had gone to watch Mickey Phelps play baseball. Friday, happily traveling in her backpack, was the big hit of the game, which as it turned out was a no-hitter for Mickey. While they were there, he had grabbed Mickey's helmet and raced up and down the bleachers with it to the delight of everyone—with the possible exception of Mickey, who was next at bat at the time. The weather had gotten warm, and Friday really enjoyed his trips outside. And now that the chimp-nappers were in custody, so did Rachel.

The first thing she noticed was her father's face. It had that look. That look of feeling sorry for her about something she didn't know about but soon would. She wondered what it could be about. The second thing she noticed was a letter in his hand. She had that feeling at the back of her neck that told her that somehow that letter was what it was about.

She slipped off her backpack, and Friday went into the living room to give Wetspot a tummy rub. Wetspot had come to expect a tummy rub every time they returned from anywhere, and Friday had become his personal masseur.

"I think you'd better read this," her father said in a way that told her right away that it was something she didn't want to read.

"It's addressed to you."

"It concerns all of us."

The letter was from Kenya, from Dee Dee VanAusdale. Rachel didn't want to read it. And when her father handed it to her and suggested that she might want to sit down, she *really* didn't want to read it. But she knew she had no choice. It was one of those no-turning-back moments, like jumping off a diving board and realizing you're going to land on your belly and it's going to hurt but it's too late to do anything about it. She sat down and began to read. She knew it was going to hurt.

Dear Ben Stelson,

On Bucky Greene's last visit to our preserve, which, of course, I never suspected would be his last (Neither did Bucky, thought Rachel), he told me he had left Mergatroid in your good care. He gave me your address in the event that anything happened to him before he was able to arrange for Mergatroid's deliverance. At the time I thought he was just being overly protective for the twins' sake—and for the sake of the life-saving information that our study of these two chimp siblings, Mergatroid and Mindy, separated at birth, may be able to provide to future generations.

I don't know how much he told you about the genetically modified bananas he was working on and their effect of enhancing intelligence. (How about *nothing!*) But from what he told me, I suspect you've probably noticed that Mergatroid is a very bright chimpanzee. (Bright enough to fool the FBI!) Yet although he has an intelligence far beyond his years, the reality remains that this is a two-and-a-half-year-old chimp with the same emotional needs as others his age. Bucky's plan was to return Mergatroid to the colony in the hope that his offspring will benefit from his DNA, possibly sparing them from the endangered species list forever.

I have made arrangements for Mergatroid to be flown here as soon as I hear from you. You must understand that time is of the essence. If he becomes too humanly imprinted, he will be unable to live among his own kind ever again.

Sincerely,
Dee Dee VanAusdale
Pampana Preserve, Kenya

"Well," said Rachel, her voice quavering, "we'll just have to tell her that we . . . we . . ." Her father put his arm around her shoulder. The unspoken tenderness and understanding of his gesture tore through her like a lightning bolt, and she burst into tears.

Friday stopped mid tummy rub and looked up. Followed by Wetspot, he crossed to where she was sitting and pushed his face up to hers. Rachel took one look at him and broke into a heartbreaking wail worthy of any of his mighty thirty-two.

My Chimp Friday

Jared emerged from his bedroom. "What's going on?"

Rachel sniffed. "It's Friday . . . ," she began, and then started to sob again.

"What's wrong with Friday?"

"Nothing's wrong with Friday," his father assured him.

"What's wrong with Rachel?"

"Well," his father said quietly, "it's Friday."

"What is it with Friday?"

Ben Stelson put his other arm around his son's shoulders. "Friday's going home."

Later that evening when she should have been asleep, Rachel sat across from Friday on her bed. The moonlight (or maybe it was the streetlight) cast a prism of white across her comforter. Friday traced the outline idly with his finger.

"I think we need to have this talk," Rachel whispered. "You see, we got this letter from—" No, that wasn't the way she wanted to put it. What she wanted to do was ask him what he wanted to do. Did he want to go—she couldn't even say the word "home" because home was here, with her. Wasn't it?

Why couldn't it be?

She looked around her room. It comforted her to gaze at the shelves crowded with family photographs and things she loved in the glow of her computer screen. There was no doubt that this was where she belonged. But was it where a chimpanzee—even an ultrasmart one—belonged?

"Oh, Friday, I want you to have a wonderful life. Do you understand that? I don't want to let you go, ever." She began to cry again. "If I could make the world different, I would. I'd make it so that when you love someone . . . a person or a pet . . . you'd always be together no matter what. But"—she blew her nose—"that's not always possible. Do you know what I mean?"

Friday stared at her with an unreadable expression.

"Do you?"

He pointed to himself. She really had confused him about who was "you" and who was "me."

"I know you would know what I mean if you could. But you can't know, can you?" She was asking and answering her own questions, but she didn't care. She suddenly realized that this was an important heart-to-heart talk—even if it was with herself.

She stroked Friday's head. "You may play solitaire on a computer, do puzzles, and eat pizza and cream cheese and jelly sandwiches, but this isn't really your world, is it?" He didn't have to answer. Rachel knew in that moment that for all she'd taught him, he'd taught her more. There was no longer any doubt in her mind that truly loving another creature meant being able to do what was best for it. She just wished she were as sure that she'd be strong enough to do it.

In the days that followed, Rachel couldn't concentrate on anything. Every time she looked at Friday, her eyes filled with tears. And when she wasn't looking at him, she was thinking about him, which wasn't any easier on her tear ducts. Her eyes looked like red-rimmed saucers. She wore sunglasses to school, telling everyone (except Mickey and Brianne, who knew the truth) that she had given Wetspot a bath with a new, specially scented, flea-repelling dog shampoo that she had discovered she was allergic to. When Rachel told a lie she gave more details than anyone wanted to hear; it kept them from asking questions. It also kept her from lying a lot. It was too much trouble.

She tried to keep her spirits up for Jared's sake—and for Friday's. He knew something was amiss and kept repeatedly trying to bring it back to normal by crawling into her lap and offering her a bite of his cream cheese and jelly sandwich. But whenever he did this it would simply underscore the fact that he was going back to the wild where there were no cream cheese and jelly sandwiches, and she'd start to weep all over again. Jared computed that if they all continued to sob and sniffle into Kleenex at the rate they were currently sobbing and sniffling into Kleenex (the "they" including their father and Mrs. Carey), they would use up "a redwood's worth of tissues." It was environmentally incorrect, something *Save the Planet* would frown on, but Rachel was too upset to care.

Dee Dee VanAusdale sent the paperwork necessary to secure a "passport" for Friday, who would be traveling under the name Mergatroid. (Rachel still couldn't understand anyone naming *anything* Mergatroid. It sounded like a liquid you drank to settle an upset stomach. And even if it were a liquid for settling upset stomachs, it should have been called something else.) Before he could leave the country for Africa, he had to have a clean bill of health, so they made an appointment with Dr. Jameson.

As they rode in the taxi across town to the Animal Medical Center, Rachel remembered speeding there two months earlier, when Friday had come down with pneumonia. It seemed so long ago. Although he had come into her life just a month after her twelfth birthday, being eleven seemed long ago, too. Friday played with her fingers, stroking them one by one as if counting them. Each felt like a razor cut to her heart.

The taxi driver was annoying and kept saying, "Wowsa!" over and over as he looked in his rearview mirror. "I ain't never had a chimp in my cab before, but I have had my share of monkeys and turkeys . . . if you know what I mean."

Rachel's father assured him that he did and, after they narrowly missed sideswiping a hot-dog vender, gently suggested that he keep his eyes on the road. Rachel and Friday turned to see the shaken vender angrily waving a frankfurter after them.

The driver saw it, too. He shook his head. "Them things will kill ya. They're just heart attacks on a roll." When they pulled up to the Animal Medical Center, he asked what was wrong with Friday.

"Nothing," said Rachel.

"Gotta be somethin' wrong." He smiled unpleasantly, exhibiting a sparse lineup of yellow teeth.

"No, there doesn't. He's fine."

"Then why you bringing him here, eh?"

"Because"—her father said seriously, handing him the fare and closing the door—"he's a hypochondriac, and we're humoring him."

Rachel loved her father's way of saying, "Put a cork in it!"

Dr. Jameson greeted Friday like an old buddy, and Friday responded with hoots of delight. "You're doing a very wise thing," he said when they explained where Friday was going. "As bright and cute as he is, he is still a wild animal who's going to get very big. You're lucky to have found a way for him to return to his natural habitat."

Rachel cast her eyes to the floor. Yeah, really lucky.

Friday was intently studying the stethoscope that was lying on the examining table, turning it over in his hands. Then he put it on, fitting the earpieces into his two comically saucer shaped ears, and pressed the silver disk against Rachel's chest.

"Well, look at that," Dr. Jameson said, shaking his head, impressed. "He's listening to your heart."

Rachel wondered if he could hear it breaking.

Hester Mundis

22.

The Saddest Part

Dee Dee VanAusdale had sent them a small, sturdy carrying case for shipping Friday in. She had explained that the less room he had to move around in, the less likely he would be tossed about in the event of turbulence, and the calmer he'd be. She'd also arranged for a flight that would more or less coincide with his bedtime, guaranteeing that she would be at the Kenya airport to greet him personally in the morning. It was a small consolation.

As much as Rachel had thought she'd prepared herself for the day of departure, when it arrived, she was a mess. So was Jared, who blubbered every time Friday hopped in the Upmobile and slid down, which had become a favorite pastime. Even Wetspot looked sad.

"If only I knew that he believed we were doing the right thing," Rachel said, sniffing and pointing. Friday was at her computer keyboard. "He's going to miss all the things he can play with here. My computer, my telephone, my backpack"—her voice broke—"me." She ran sobbing from the room.

When her father announced it was time to leave for the

airport, Rachel grabbed a fistful of tissues and shoved them in her pocket. She knew she was going to need them. She took her soft, flannel Dahl School sweatshirt and put it inside the carrying case that Friday would be traveling in. He liked feeling snuggly. Jared handed her a box of raisins, and she put that in, too. Friday studied the case, crawling inside, opening and closing the door and examining the latch. "Don't even think about it," Rachel said, and for the first time that day, she sort of smiled. Sort of.

"We'd better get going."

Friday hooted excitedly. He knew he was going somewhere. But would he be as excited if he knew where? And that he wasn't coming back? She didn't want to think about it, and she couldn't stop thinking about it. If only she could think of something that would help take her mind off it.

She looked around the room quickly. Where was her Rubik's Cube? "Jared, have you seen my Rubik's Cube?"

"No."

"Rachel. We have to leave," her father called.

She rummaged through her backpack, looked under the bed, on her desk, and in the Upmobile, but it wasn't there. So much for being a *lucky* charm. She silently vowed that when she found it she was going to smash it into confetti-sized chips and flush them down the toilet!

"Ra-chel!"

She grabbed more tissues and carried an excited Friday in her arms out of the apartment for the last time.

The ride to the airport was excruciatingly (e-x-c-r-u-c-i-a-t-i-n-g-l-y) painful. Every time Friday looked out the window and burst into excited "uh-uh-uhs," either Rachel or Jared burst into tears.

When they pulled into the parking lot, Friday climbed

into Rachel's lap and wiped two fresh drops from her cheek with his finger and tasted them. "If you . . . if you . . . if you . . . ," she stammered. Friday pointed proudly to himself. "If you could just tell me that you were going to be all right."

Friday scratched his head. Then he puckered his lips and kissed her. It would have to do.

Inside the terminal, as her father made arrangements with the airline attendant in charge of transporting animals, Friday wiggled from Rachel's arms and began doing somersaults on one of the baggage carousels. Rachel didn't have the heart to curtail him. He looked like a fuzzy piece of round luggage having fun. Several flight attendants pulling wheeled suitcases behind them stopped and became the fuzzy piece of round luggage's responsive audience. Wild animal or not, Friday was a ham. When the attendants applauded, he bowed like a courtier (he'd seen *The Three Musketeers* on television), then he hunkered over to each of them and shook hands.

And then it was time. Rachel's father put the carrying case down in front of her. It was an attractive, sturdy brown case with nice round windows and a neatly screened door. Rachel felt sick to her stomach when she looked at it. She swallowed hard and took Friday's hand and, as he waved good-bye to his audience, she walked him to his traveling compartment and opened the door. He saw the sweatshirt, gave a lusty "hoo-hoo" (the train whistle), and went right in. Her father fastened the latch.

Friday fell silent and stuck his hand out the case window. Rachel knelt down and held it, tears streaming down her face. "You'll be all right. I just wish you knew it now."

There was a soft "hoo-hoo."

Jared patted Friday's hand, sniffing back tears. "We'll

My Chimp Friday

miss you. Wetspot will, too. He loved your tummy rubs a lot."

Rachel and Jared sat on the floor with Friday until the attendant told them it was time to take him on board. They kissed him good-bye, and cried openly as he was carried away. Rachel never knew the human body contained so many tears.

She was drained when they returned from the airport. She threw herself facedown on her comforter, too weak to utter another sob. If only she knew he'd be all right. If only he knew that she didn't want to give him up. If only she could have explained to him why he was being sent away and be certain he understood. If only . . . after about ten minutes of self-torturing "if onlys," she sighed and sat up. She didn't like to bother God with little things, things that weren't matters of life or death, but it couldn't hurt to just this once ask for a small favor. She clasped her hands and was about to ask God to give her a sign that they had made the right decision, when she noticed that her computer was on. Friday had been playing with it before they left. As she went to turn it off, she saw there was writing on the screen. She stared at it and couldn't stop staring at it.

It was unbelievable. It was incredible. It was from Friday.

What it said filled her heart with such joy that she started sobbing all over again. The pronouns were wrong, but the message could not have been more right.

"ME NO CRY. YOU HAPPY TO GO HOME."

She pressed the SAVE button on her computer, but she didn't have to.

Hester Mundis

23.

Jungling for Joy

When the phone rang the following morning, Rachel heard her father say Dee Dee's name and dashed to his side. He patted the air, signaling her to calm down and let him listen.

"He did? Really? Why, that's wonderful."

"He did what?" Rachel asked eagerly, bouncing up and down a lot like Friday. "What's wonderful?"

Her father shushed her. "Yes, yes . . ."

"What? What?"

He shot her a not-so-saintly patient look. It was his one-raised-eyebrow first-alert warning. She pretended to zip her lip.

There were a lot of "uh-huhs" and "ums" from her father, which were very annoying because they gave her absolutely no clue about what was being said.

"That's my daughter's doing," he said, laughing.

"What's my doing?"

Her father held up his hand. Rachel rolled her head, exasperated. One would think that if people are talking about you, you have a right to know what they are saying while they are saying it! For the first time in her life, she harrumphed indignantly. Unfortunately, it came out like a belch. Her father shot her a surprised look, and she mumbled, "Excuse me."

"At first sight, eh? We'd love to see them. Can you e-mail it?" There was a pause, and her father gave Dee Dee their e-mail address.

Waiting to hear the other side of a phone conversation was always annoying. Waiting to hear the other side of this one was unbearable. She was practically choking with curiosity. She wanted to know all the details immediately. What was Dee Dee going to e-mail?

"I certainly will, and I know she'll be very happy to hear it. Good-bye." Rachel's father was smiling as he hung up.

"Well?"

"She said his flight arrived on time, and he enjoyed the movie."

"DADDY!" Sometimes her father picked the worst times to attempt being funny. "Come on. What did she really say? Is Friday all right? Did he meet his sister? Is he happy? Do they like him?"

"He was welcomed by the group with open arms— which Dee Dee said was very surprising since this is rarely the case with new arrivals. Then she saw that the open-arm welcome was because he was handing out raisins."

"Leave it to our Friday."

Jared, who'd joined them, said, "Wow. Chimps in the wild really are different. When he lived here he never shared those raisins."

"She also said that, remarkably, he doesn't seem to have been too humanly imprinted, because in less than an hour he had learned how to groom other chimps."

"When he was here, he learned to play solitaire in less than an hour."

"That's not the point," their father said. "If he had become too humanly imprinted, too used to our ways, he wouldn't be able to relate to his own kind. He wouldn't have the company of his natural sister and the chance for close personal contact with other chimpanzees. He wouldn't have been able to be happy in that world. And he would never be accepted as an equal in ours. As uniquely intelligent as he is, he is nonetheless an ape who deserves the fullest possible life. He is a noble animal. Our closest living relative. He was never meant to be a pet. To deny him his birthright would be very wrong." He smiled at Rachel. "Dee Dee said to thank you for all you've done for him."

Rachel swallowed hard. "I . . . I'm glad. I only wish that I could see for myself that he really is enjoying himself."

"You will. Dee Dee said she would e-mail a picture right away."

"Do you think she did it already?"

"Possibly."

Rachel and Jared turned and ran into Rachel's bedroom and turned on the computer. Rachel crossed her fingers. Please be there.

"You've got mail," said the computer.

There it was. "Subject: Mergatroid. Sender: Dee Dee VanAusdale."

Rachel opened the letter. There was a note from Dee Dee and an attachment.

"I think this photo is worth a thousand words. And Mergatroid is worth a thousand thank-yous. With his help we can save this increasingly endangered species."

Rachel clicked on the attachment, and slowly the photo

began to appear on the screen. "Look," she cried, "there he is!"

And there he was, happily hanging from a branch with one arm, opposite another chimp who was doing the same (and who looked remarkably like him). His mouth was open in a huge, full-crescent grin. And partly concealed in his other hand, but glinting in the sunlight so that the colors were unmistakable, was her missing Rubik's Cube!

Rachel felt bubbles of happiness swell in her chest. That little devil! That wonderful, adorable, light-fingered imp. Friday had gone home, but he had taken a piece of her world with him.

She no longer had any doubt that he was where he belonged—and that wherever he was, he would always be in her heart.

Hester Mundis

Boris, the inspiration for Friday, with Hester Mundis's nine-year-old son, Shep, in 1969.

David Sagarin

Author's Note

Once upon a time there was a real chimp named Boris. He was raised by a family in a Manhattan apartment for nearly three years. They loved him desperately. They loved him enough to come to realize that although he had been taken out of the jungle, he didn't belong in a city. He was an ape—a noble wild creature—and was never meant to be domesticated. They loved him enough to understand that what he needed—and deserved—was a home among his own. As heart-wrenching a decision as it was to make, it was the right one. I know, because I've never regretted it.

Boris was the inspiration for this book. Today, he is the dominant chimp of his colony, the father of twelve, and continues to thrive with the companionship of his species on an island habitat without bars at the Chester Zoological Gardens in Chester, England.